A History of Bridgeburg and Its People

BOB WHITED

Copyright © 2020 Bob Whited
All rights reserved
First Edition

PAGE PUBLISHING, INC.
Conneaut Lake, PA

First originally published by Page Publishing 2020

ISBN 978-1-6624-2230-0 (pbk)
ISBN 978-1-6624-2231-7 (digital)

Printed in the United States of America

Other Books by Bob Whited

Navy Grass, a memoir of the author's time spent in the US Navy

Bridgeburg Maple

Transplanted some fifty years ago as a sapling to my front yard in Austintown, Ohio, from the grounds of the Bridgeburg School.

This book is dedicated to my late brother, Lawrence "Larry" E. Whited (08-28-1939 to 08-09-2016). Before his death, Larry asked me to write this history. Hopefully, he would be pleased with the resulting narrative.

Thank you for your idea and inspiration, Larry. It's been fun!

INTRODUCTION

On writing a history of Bridgeburg, a small hamlet in Western Pennsylvania, Armstrong County, East Franklin Township, two features immediately emerge. They are the beautiful Allegheny River and the huge railroad bridge that spans the river from West Mosgrove/Bridgeburg to Mosgrove. The railroad bridge was opened in 1899 with the BR&P (Buffalo, Rochester, and Pittsburgh) Railroad.

But the river itself made everything happen, from the early Indian tribes to the early settlers and, of course, the magnificent railroad bridge itself that came much later. Along with the bridge came the growth of the railroad industry, which made this giant bridge not only possible, but also necessary.

In this narrative, we will explore the many families and their origins who settled in this small town, their contributions, their industries, and their simple way of life. We will also explore the history and the building of the great railroad bridge coinciding with the constant background of the Allegheny River.

Photo courtesy of Harry Gaydosz.

CHAPTER 1

History and the River

The Allegheny River was described by the French as *la belle riviere* or "the beautiful river." This river has a very illustrious history on its own—first, with several Indian tribes, mainly the Delaware or Lenape and the Shawnee then the French and the English or British. The Shawnee and the Delaware appeared to have settled along the Allegheny as early as 1719.

We all know somewhat of the flowing of this river that extends onward in a long journey, approximately three hundred fifteen miles, starting in Colesburg, Pennsylvania, then meandering to Coudersport, turning north into the state of New York, flowing past the city of Salamanca, west of Warren, Pennsylvania, and proceeding southward, ending in Pittsburgh, Pennsylvania, where it joins the Monongahela River to form the Ohio River. On its way south, it flows past Kittanning or Kithane, a former Delaware or Lenape Indian village, which was the site of a historical setting and great battle in the French and Indian wars. Just approximately five miles north of Kittanning is the scene of our story.

The village of Mosgrove sits on the east side of the river. Bridgeburg, formerly known as West Mosgrove, was settled on the west side of the river. Most early American settlements were founded close to a river. This was no exception for the settlements that grew up along the winding Allegheny River. They were first inhabited by several Native American or Indian tribes. The settlers used the river and its many tributaries for many resources including fishing and hunting and, of course, trading.

Rivers at that time were used for transportation and carriage of goods from one settlement or Indian village to the other, using barter or trade as a means of survival. The fur trade was always abundant and resourceful.

After all was said and done, the Delaware sect of the Lenape nation became residents of our area of discussion and proclaimed Kittanning or Kithane as their home, some five miles south of our story's scene on both the east and west banks of the Allegheny.

In those early days during the eighteenth century, both the French and the British wanted a foothold on what, at that time, was referred to as the Ohio country, which also included the Western Pennsylvania area. The French wanted all the action that they could obtain through trading with the different tribes while trying to push the British out and have it all, including the lands.

The French and the British were never very friendly with each other. From 1744–1748 they were involved in what was referred to as King George's War, which never settled much or any of their land disputes.

The French finally gave an aggressive movement for the possession of the Ohio Valley. On June 15, 1749, they decided to send a flotilla of large boats and canoes under the command of Celeron de Bienville from Montreal along with some two hundred twenty French and Canadians with, perhaps, another sixty

Indians to ascend the Allegheny. The trek down the river included leaving lead plates along the way, printed in French, proclaiming that they had possession of all those lands.

To this day, researchers and searchers continue looking for those plates as some of them have been found. This flotilla went the whole way down the Allegheny and into the Ohio River and beyond. The flotilla never seemed to prove a point until the French and Indian wars erupted a few years later in 1754. With the defeat of George Washington and his Virginia militia at Fort Necessity on July 3, 1754, and General Braddock's terrible defeat close to Fort Duquesne on July 9, 1755, it seems to foretell a very difficult time for the British and our American colonists.

As the French and Indian wars continued, Kittanning or Kithane became a hot spot with the Delawares led by Shingas and Tewea, or Captain Jacobs as he was also called. These leaders of the Western Delaware tribe dwelled there in their village of Kithane and embraced the French. After many raids by the Delawares and the killing and capture of many farmers, women, and children, Colonel John Armstrong was selected to raise an army of rangers and attack the Kittanning village. On September 8, 1756, along with some two hundred ninety rangers, Colonel Armstrong made a raid at dawn with a battle that took many hours to complete, but became victorious. Armstrong himself was wounded. Tewea, or Captain Jacobs, and his family were killed among much rifle fire with a background of huge explosions of kegs of black powder that exploded during the torching of the village and the cabins.

Shingas was absent from the attack and continued on the warpath. There were some eleven captives who were freed and welcomed by Armstrong's rangers.

Armstrong in later years served in the Continental Army and the Continental Congress. His reward for all his service was a huge track of land (some five hundred fifty acres) along the Allegheny River, of all places. Armstrong County is named after him.

A view of the Allegheny River from our home.

CHAPTER 2

Forming Armstrong County and East Franklin and Rayburn Townships

It seems forming settlements did not happen until after the final fear of Indian uprisings, the end of the French and Indian conflict, and our own war for independence. Armstrong County was formed in 1800 from parts of Allegheny, Lycoming, and Westmoreland counties. The years 1800–1825 were thought of as improvement years as homes sprang up replacing many log cabins. Farmers were again plowing their fields and enjoying life as never before without fear.

East Franklin Township, named after Benjamin Franklin, was settled in 1830 and incorporated in 1868. It is located in west-central Armstrong County on the west side of the Allegheny River.

It now surrounds the boroughs of West Kittanning and Applewold. It also includes unincorporated communities of West Hills, Walkchalk, Furnace Run, Tarrtown, Bridgeburg, Adrian, and Cowansville.

Mosgrove is situated directly across the river from Bridgeburg / West Mosgrove in Rayburn Township. Rayburn Township was named after a Judge Rayburn. Mosgrove was named after a famous landowner and furnaceman, James B. Mosgrove, who built the Pine Creek Furnace. James Lowry opened a store near the mouth of Pine Creek in 1852. The first official post office in Mosgrove was not opened until October 1, 1904.

Bob Whited

(Reference map from 1876.)

CHAPTER 3

Early Settlers and Families in Bridgeburg (West Mosgrove)

At present, I have not found out when or who changed the name of West Mosgrove to Bridgeburg. It may be noted that the BR&P (Buffalo, Rochester, and Pittsburgh) Railroad Bridge was completed in 1899. Being that this was a major achievement for this small area and it was also a giant bridge, it is understandable that the name of Bridgeburg stands out more so than West Mosgrove and was so renamed.

Some of the first families to settle in this Bridgeburg area will now be somewhat explored. I tried to get all families correct. The following early families are the ones most remembered by me.

James Patton Sr. Family

The James Patton Sr. family was probably one of the first families to settle in West Mosgrove. James was born on June 19, 1794, and his death was on December 2, 1871. James was buried in the Myers-Patton Cemetery in Bridgeburg. The family was originally from Ireland. Jane Sloan-Patton (1799–1877) was his spouse. Their children were Montgomery Patton (1819–1881), John Sloan Patton (1821–1902), Thomas Patton (1826–1885), William R. Patton, my great-grandfather (1831—1881), and Samuel H. Patton (1835–1914).

My great-grandfather William R. Patton's claim to fame was being in the California Gold Rush of 1849. There have been many stories concerning his trek to the goldfields and who accompanied him and even of him striking gold. However, I have not been able to find out for sure if he really did find gold or how much he struck it rich. There are many stories of this, but we may never know the real truth.

William R's spouse was Sarah Ann Swigart-Patton (1837–1915). Their children were Marion Loren Patton (1864–1956), Laura Jane Patton-Whited, my grandmother (1866–1913), Alonia Patton-Selder (1868–1941), Frank J. Patton (1872–1916), Norman Gilpin "Gilp" Patton (1874–1948), Mary A. Patton-Slagle (1876–1942), and Lawrence Tilden "Orie" Patton (1879–1951).

Their farm was well-known for its crystal clear and cold spring water that was unbelievable. Years later, Haws Refractories used this water to create a reservoir and produce running water to not only the brickyard, but many households in the area as well. The water, which we all enjoyed for many years, was piped to our home. The Patton farm was located directly west of the River Road close to a half mile. The setting was beautiful.

Some photos are shown here of Sarah Patton, Marion, Frank, and Gilpin and Alonia Patton, along with the reservoir and the early Patton homestead. The Patton family was known to be great builders and farmers, especially the family of Thomas Patton.

Alonia Patton (daughter of Sarah and William Patton) & Walter Selders

Frank Patton family (son of Sarah and William Patton). Sons, William and Baxter.

The Reservoir June 1955

Sarah Swigart-Patton

Marion Patton (Sarah's & William R's son)

Gilpin Patton (Sarah's & William R.'s son)

Original William R. Patton home circa late 1980s.

Bob Whited at the reservoir, July 1967.

John Wesley Whited Family

Laura Jane Patton (1866–1913) married John Wesley Whited (1863–1953) in 1885, and their children were Sadie Irene Whited-Cloak (1885–1969), John Loren Whited (1887–1963), Pearle Blanche Whited-Elgin (1890–1925), Norman Whited (1893–1894), Laura Edna Whited-Hooks (1895–1968), Clarence Leas Whited (1898–1962), Hazel Marie Whited (1901–1976), Carl Wesley Whited (1904–1988), Elnora "Nora" Whited (1907–1969), and Elvin Otto "Webb" Whited (May 3, 1910, to April 29, 1991), who was my father.

John Wesley was the son of Henry Whited and Sarah Jane Flenner-Whited. He had two siblings, Mary "Molly" Whited-Leas and Ellie Whited. He was the grandson of John A. Whited and Mary Sheckler-Whited. John A. Whited was a veteran of the War of 1812 and was present at the Battle at Fort McHenry when our national anthem was written. John Wesley also was the great-grandson of Thomas Whited, a Revolutionary War soldier, and Mary Waters-Whited. They were from Broad Top near Bedford, Pennsylvania. John Wesley was born at Ore Hill Furnace, close to Mosgrove, Pennsylvania. Later he was an orphan living with the McCracken family because of the death of his father.

Sarah Jane Flenner-Whited-Bowser-McElravy

Mary (Molly) Whited-Leas (daughter of Sarah Jane and Henry Whited).

John Wesley Whited.

Laura Jane Patton-Whited.

Sadie Whited-Cloak.

Pearle Blanche Whited-Elgin

1938 TAX NOTICE FOR EAST FRANKLIN TOWNSHIP

VALUATION: $ 450

2 Mills County		91
3½ Mills County Road Bond	1	57
1½ Mills County Poor		68
4 Mills Personal Property		
Total	3	16
5 per cent. Discount		
5 per cent. Added		
Total		
12 Mills School	3	66
Per Capita (School)	$5	00
5 Per Cent. Added		
Total		

County and Personal Property Taxes: 5% Discount until Sept 30, 1938. Face until December 31, 1938. 5% penalty thereafter.

School Tax: No Discount. 5% Penalty after October 5, 1938.

ALL TAXES MUST BE PAID BY JANUARY 1, 1939

Bring this Statement With You and Save Time

I will be at:—
Cowansville—Mateer & Smith Store, Sept. 19.
Walk Chalk—Store, Sept. 20.
Montgomeryville—Hooks' Store, Sept. 21.
West Kittanning—Vensel's Garage, Sept. 22.
Tarrtown, Sept. 23.
Mosgrove, Sept. 26.
After that at my home, Cowansville, Pa.

IF YOU DESIRE RECEIPT ENCLOSE SELF-ADDRESSED STAMPED ENVELOPE

W. S. HELM, Cowansville, Pa.

1943 TAX NOTICE for EAST FRANKLIN TOWNSHIP

Valuation: Property $ [illegible] **Occupation $** [illegible]

2 mills County		70
3 mills County Road Bond	1	05
1 mill County Poor		35
4 mills Personal Property		
Total	2	10
5 per cent Discount		
5 per cent Added		
Total		
3 mills Township Road	1	05
13 mills School	2	60
Per Capita (School)	5	00
5 per cent Added		
Total		

COUNTY ROAD and PERSONAL TAXES: 5% Discount until Sept. 30, 1943. Face until Dec 31, 1943. 5% penalty thereafter

SCHOOL and PER CAPITA TAX: No discount. 5% penalty after Sept. 30, 1943.

PROPERTY TAXES NOT PAID BEFORE MAY 1, 1944

will be returned to the County Commissioners for Collection

I will be at:
Cowansville—At home, Sept. 16.
Walk Chalk—Store, Sept. 25.
Montgomeryville—Hooks' Store, Sept. 21.
West Kittanning—Vensel's Garage, Sept. 18.
Tarrtown, Sept. 23.
Mosgrove, Sept. 27.
After that at my home, Cowansville, Pa.

W. S. HELM, Cowansville, Pa.

BRING THIS STATEMENT WITH YOU AND SAVE TIME

IF YOU DESIRE RECEIPT ENCLOSE SELF-ADDRESSED STAMPED ENVELOPE

August 1, 1951

1951 TAX NOTICE for EAST FRANKLIN TOWNSHIP

Valuation: Property $ 250 **Occupation $**

5 mills County — Real Estate	1	25
" " Occupation		
1 mill Institution — Real Estate		25
" Occupation		
4 mills Personal Property		
5 mills Twp. Road — Real Estate	1	25
" " Occupation		
18 mills School — Real Estate	4	50
Per Capita (School)	~~10~~	~~00~~
Total	7	25
2 per cent Discount		
5 per cent Added		
Total		

ALL TAXES—2% discount until Oct. 1, 1951. Face to Dec. 1, 1951. 5% penalty thereafter.

Property Taxes not paid before May 1, 1952 will be returned to the County Commissioners for collection

Collector will be at:
ADRIAN, Thursday, Sept. 13th, 9 to 12 a.m. & 1 to 5 p.m.
COWANSVILLE, Friday, Sept. 14th, 9 to 12 a.m. & 1 to 5 p.m.
WALK CHALK,
Gaiser's Store, Monday, Sept. 17th, 9 to 12 a.m. & 1 to 5 p.m.
Ritchey's Store, Tues., Sept. 18th, 9 to 12 a.m & 1 to 5 p.m.
WEST KITTANNING,
Stull's Garage, Thurs., Sept. 20th, 9 to 12 a. m. & 1 to 5 p.m.
TARRTOWN, Friday, Sept. 21st, 9 to 12 a.m. & 1 to 5 p.m.
RESIDENCE, Sept. 24th, 25th, 26th, 27th, 12 noon to 6 p.m.

T. A. SNYDER, TAX COLLECTOR, R. D. 3, KITTANNING, PA.

IF YOU DESIRE RECEIPT ENCLOSE SELF-ADDRESSED STAMPED ENVELOPE

BRING THIS STATEMENT WITH YOU AND SAVE TIME

Tax notices for John Wesley Whited.

Laura Blanche "Sis" Elgin-Anderson (05-24-1938 to 05-24-2020), granddaughter of Pearle Blanche Whited-Elgin.

Edward Elgin (grandson of Pearle Blanche Whited-Elgin.

Carolyn Elgin-Barnett (08-11-1941 to 08-29-2016), granddaughter of Pearle Blanche Whited-Elgin.

Alma Cloak-Reefer with husband,
Carl Reefer. Daughter of Sadie
Whited-Cloak and Harry Cloak.

Violet Cloak-Cousins. Married Bert Cousins. Daughter
of Sadie Whited-Cloak and Harry Cloak.

Laura Edna Whited-Hooks remained in Bridgeburg. She married Hugh A. Hooks. Their children were Laura Ruby Hooks-Freeman (01-01-1916 to 02-19-2001), Harold A. "Wood" Hooks (06-24-1917 to 11-18-1940), Lester "Leck" Hooks (05-07-1919 to 03-05-2007), and Jack Hooks (1927 to).

Hazel Marie Whited remained in Bridgeburg. Nora Whited also remained in Bridgeburg.

Laura Ruby Hooks-Freeman.

Harold "Wood" Hooks

Lester Hooks.

Jack Hooks at age sixteen. Jack used to sing on the radio station WKIN in Kittanning, PA

Elnora Whited, Frank Hockenberry, Clair Cloak, and Hazel Whited.

Hazel M. Whited.

Hazel Whited, Mrs. Sloan, Jane Cochran, and Laura Edna Whited-Hooks.

Laura Edna Hooks' home today.

Carl W. Whited remained in Bridgeburg. He married Catherine Smith-Whited (04-09-1907 to 06-18-2002). Their children were Betty Jean Whited-Rood, who married John Rood of Michigan, and they had six children, Timothy, Cathy, John, Patricia, Ricky, and Craig; William W. "Bud" Whited, who married Eva Mae Turner-Whited; and Doris Whited-Wolfe, who married Laverne Wolfe, and they had three children.

(Back) Cass Whited, Betty Whited, and Webb and Carl Whited.
(Front) Doris Whited-Wolfe, Flora May Stockdale, and Bob Whited.

Betty Whited-Rood.   William "Bud" Whited.   Doris Whited-Wolfe.

Catherine "Cass" Smith-Whited.

Carl Whited.

Doris Whited-Wolfe and Betty Whited-Rood.

Cass Whited holding Barbara Crissman.

Laverne Wolfe, spouse of Doris Whited-Wolfe.

Elvin "Webb" O. Whited remained in Bridgeburg. He married Winifred Madge Moors-Whited (06-17-1913 to 09-11-1998). Their children were Ronald E. Whited (1934–1934); Lawrence E. Whited (08-28-1939 to 08-09-2016), who married Loretta Doyle-Whited, and they had three children; and Robert D. Whited (8/14/1941), who married Joyce Toussaint-Whited, and they had four children.

A History of Bridgeburg and Its People

Webb Whited and Larry Whited.

Webb and Madge Moors-Whited.

Madge Whited.

Larry Whited.

Bob Whited.

Thomas Patton Family

For me, growing up in this community, I was always in awe of this family. Thomas Patton was born on September 10, 1826, and died on October 19, 1885. He married Elizabeth Bossinger-Patton (1825–1885). On his headstone in the Myers-Patton Cemetery is the story that relates how he was murdered while trying to save his neighbor's boat oars from being stolen by river pirates. History indicates that he was a farmer and builder.

Their children were Magdaline Patton, or Lainie as she was called (1860–1937), William "Will" Patton (1862–1949), Montgomery Patton (1865–1949), Olive "Ollie" Patton-Montgomery (1867–1954), George Bossinger "Boss" Patton (1869–1954), and James C. Patton (1871–1955).

Will was a great builder and was renowned for his work throughout Pennsylvania and beyond. Montgomery was also a great builder. The Patton family maintained a sawmill and quarried their own stone directly across the river in Mosgrove along Pine Creek. Mont (as Montgomery was called) met his death while repairing a slate roof atop the home of Carl Whited. George, or Boss when I knew him, lived in a shantyboat directly across the River Road from the main family home. Some say that shantyboat was originally a ferryboat that transported people across the river before the bridge was built. Who knows? Perhaps, a falling out with the rest of his family directed him to live on the boat, or he just preferred living alone. Their main house was built close to the river on the River Road.

Most people are unaware that Boss was a hero in the early Johnstown (Pennsylvania) Flood on May 31, 1889. Being an expert oarsman, he saved many lives as a boatman answering the call in this great emergency. As a baby, I contracted whooping cough and nearly died. Boss rowed my mother and me across the river through ice to get us on the train and to the Kittanning Hospital. Again, Boss' expert boatmanship, perhaps, saved my life. Boss was married to Mary A. McCracken-Patton on September 18, 1888, and was widowed. They had two children—a son, Audith Patton (1888–1941), who served in World War I, and a daughter, Elmo Patton-Donaldson (1891–1920).

Audith Patton, son of George Bossinger Patton and Mary McCracken-Patton

Original Thomas Patton family house as it is today.

Pennsylvania, WWI Veterans Service and Compensation Files, 1917-...
Army   Patterson, Albert - Paulick, John J (335)

as authorized by Act No. 53, approved January 5, 1934; I was a resident of Pennsylvania at time of entry into service; I make this claim with full knowledge of the penalty for making a false statement relative to a material fact concerning this claim and the answers to the following questions and descriptive information are true:

(2) PATTON   AUDITH   417045   WHITE
    (Last name) (First and middle name) (Serial number) (White or colored)

(3) Legal residence at entry into service 1036 LEISHMAN AVE., NEW KENSINGTON, WESTMORLAND CO PA
    (Street and number, City, County and State)

(4) Present residence: 1300 NORTH WATER ST., KITTANNING, PA (ARMSTRONG COUNTY)
    (Street and number, City, County and State)

(5) Enlisted, commissioned or inducted in RA; ANC, NA, NG, ERC, Navy, NRF, MC, ORC, Pa. Vols, US Vols; at
    NEW KENSINGTON, PA.   on MAY 3, 1918

(6) On active duty in Navy or in Reserve from _____ to _____

(7) Place and date of birth EAST FRANKLIN TOWNSHIP, ARMSTRONG COUNTY, PA.

(8) Names and addresses of dependents: Wife (full name) NONE
    Minor children NONE
    Mother (full name) DECEASED
    Father PATTON, GEORGE BOSSINGER   Mosgrove, Pa.

(9) Service in organizations, at stations or on vessels in the order named as follows:
    PVT. CO. D. 54th. INFANTRY   from MAY 3, 1918   to MAY 2, 1919.
                                   from _____   to _____
                                   from _____   to _____

(10) Grades or ratings with dates of appointments or promotions: none
(11) Engagements: none
(12) Wounds or other injuries received with dates: none

Audith Patton service file

Lawrence Tilden "Orie" Patton Family

Lawrence Tilden "Orie" Patton (1879–1951) and his family chose to remain on the farm and properties of his late father, William R. Patton, in Bridgeburg. He married Annie Catherine Hooks-Patton (1882–1948) in 1901. Their children were Goldie Ruth Patton-Aiken (1901–1980), Florence B. Patton (1902–1977), Harry Andrew Patton (1904–1971), Sara Mae Patton-Zeigler (1906–1993), Roxie Patton-Dailey (1908–1991), Laura Edna Patton-Lash (1910–1987), Wilda Patton-Shaffer (1912–1981), Mary Patton-Innes (1915–2003), Adda Melissa Patton-Lemmon (1918–2014), Lawrence Homer Patton (1920–1970), and Gladys A. Patton-Rice (1922–2013).

Florence Patton.

Orie Patton *(left)*, Jacob A. Tarr *(middle)*, and other person not identified.

Laura Edna Patton married Russel "Ding" Lash and remained in Bridgeburg. Their children were Russel Dwight "Sonny" Lash, Charles Lash, Ellen Lash-Toy, and Glee Lash-Lawrence.

Charles Lash.

Ellen Lash-Toy.

Glee Lash-Lawrence.

Ellen Lash-Toy with dog, Springer.

Wilda Patton-Shaffer married Henry "Boo" Shaffer and remained in Bridgeburg. Their children were Paul Steele Shaffer, Robert Wallas Shaffer, Donald "Junior" Shaffer, and Gene P. Shaffer.

Gene P. Shaffer.

Samuel H. Patton Family

Samuel H. Patton was born in August 1835 and was the son of James Patton Sr. and Jane Sloan-Patton. He married Catherine M. Tarr (02-1843–) in 1868. Their children were Alfaretta Patton-Cloak (06-10-1868 to 03-14-1939), Ida Almira "Miley" Patton-Flatt (03-11-1870 to 12-05-1964), Jane "Jennie" Patton-Cochran (1876–1967), James AG Patton (09-1881–).

Jane "Jennie" Patton married James Marlin "Casey" Cochran (03-09-1871 to 10-16-1949) on April 20, 1915, and remained in Bridgeburg. Their children were Robert, Harold, Mildred Lucille Cochran-Peoples, Raymond, and Roy. We all knew Jane very well and her friendliness to all of us kids. Casey and their son, Bob, would hook up an amusement-park train on their property, and we used to ride the train—fond memories. Bob also had a giant, antique steam engine.

Samuel H. Patton was the son of James Patton Sr. and Jane Sloan-Patton. Their farm was located on the east side and west side of the Shawmut Railroad, close to the river, and east of the River Road.

Jenny Jane Cochran.

Bob Cochran with his steam engine.

Bob, Harold, and Roy Cochran.

The Solomon Hooks Family

Solomon Hooks was born on March 28, 1826, and passed on December 15, 1900. His spouse was Susanna Crissman-Hooks (1832–1901). Their children were William Henry Hooks (1852–1926), Cyrus Chambers Hooks (1853–1931), John Y. Hooks (1858–1939), Sharon Quigley Hooks (1859–1915), Jacob Elmer Hooks (1865–1910), Ida Florence Hooks-Wolff (1870–1956), Mary Hooks-Bowser (1872–1959), and Rebecca Patton Hooks-Lasher (1875–1966).

JY Hooks Family

JY Hooks married Elizabeth Ritchey-Hooks (1866–1946). He decided to stay and farm in West Mosgrove/Bridgeburg. Their children were Ralph Waldo Hooks (1891–1965), Chauncey Depew Hooks (1897–1970), Charles Edgar Hooks (1893–1933), Theodore Henry Hooks (1900–1974), Mary L. Hooks-Beatty (1907–2003), Raymond Hooks, Bessie Hooks-Bowser (1890–), Annabell Hooks-McIlwain, and Eva Hooks-Williams (1896–).

Ralph W. Hooks.

Ralph W. Hooks.

Mary Hooks

Eva Hooks.

Bessie Hooks.

Bessie Hooks-Bowser.

Theodore Henry Hooks Sr. resided on his father's farm after the death of his parents. He married Ruth Galvin-Hooks (1912–1985), and their children included Elizabeth "Teet" Hooks-Rupp, Alice "Tine" Hooks-Cogley, Jean Hooks-Toy, and Theodore H. Hooks Jr., who was a good friend of mine. This family was always close to me while growing up, and they were always friendly and great fun as well.

Theodore H. Hooks Jr., Junior as he was always called, was born on May 9, 1939, and passed away on May 19, 2010. He remained on the Hooks farm in Bridgeburg. He was married to Nancy Campbell-Hooks. Their children were Tammy Hooks-Henry, Theodore Hooks III, Wanda Hooks-Haley, Brenda Hooks-Kennedy, and April Hooks-Johns.

Ruth Galvin-Hooks.

Elizabeth "Teet" Hooks-Rupp.

Jean Hooks-Toy.

Ted "Junior" Hooks.

J Y Hooks home as it is today

Myers Family

William T. Myers (1827–1889) married Elizabeth J. Swigart-Myers (1835–1874). Their son, Abraham Gilpen "AG" Myers (1872–1955), married Elizabeth Anna Roofner-Myers (1875–1943). They lived on a farm along the Quigley Hill Road. Their children were Eva Jane Myers-Reddinger (1894–1969), Flora Mildred Myers-Zellefrow (1895–1970), Myrtle Mae Myers-Farester (1897–1950), Thomas G. Myers (1899–1974), Lloyd S. Myers (1901–1928), Margaret Elizabeth Myers-Beighley (1903–1983), Infant Myers (1904–1904), Ida Irene Myers-Lasher-Zimmerman (1905–1983), John B. Myers (1907–1989, his son, Lloyd, was a good friend of mine), Jesse Monroe Myers (1911–1985), Paul Woodrow Myers (1913–2005), and Pluma Wilhemina Myers-Claypoole (1915–1997), who married Chambers "Cub" Claypoole.

Margaret Myers *(left)*, Hazel Whited *(center)*, and others unidentified.

Flora Myers married Lee Zellefrow, and Ida Irene Myers-Lasher later married Elmer Zimmerman, and they remained residents of West Mosgrove / Bridgeburg. Flora's children were Randall and Lloyd George Zellefrow and Constance Zellefrow-Cousins. Lloyd A. Myers was also raised by Flora and Lee Zellefrow.

Ida Irene Myers-Lasher later married Elmer Zimmerman and eventually moved to the Ford City area. Avanell Lasher Painter and Ronald Lasher were her children. Ronald was a good friend of mine. Avanell married Homer Painter.

A History of Bridgeburg and Its People

Ronald Lasher.

Lloyd A. Myers.

(Left–right) Lloyd Myers and Ron Lasher.

Henry Rebold Family

Henry Rebold was born on November 11, 1845, in Ladder Hesse, Germany, and passed in 1926. He married Margaret Kollar-Rebold in 1872 in East Franklin Township, Armstrong County, Pennsylvania. Their children were John H. Rebold, Julia Ann Rebold-Heinrich, Margaret M. Rebold-Steffey, Sarah Rebold, Alice Emma Rebold, Catherine Annie Rebold-Gray, and George Lee Rebold. Their farm adjoined the Thomas Patton and the JY Hooks farms. The Rebold Hill was always a sight to see when growing up in Bridgeburg, especially when the sheep were grazing. George Rebold stayed on the farm.

George Lee Rebold (1888–1976) married Lena Bell Toy-Rebold (1894–1982). Their children were Ivy L. Rebold-Patton (1919–2002), Leslie Henry Rebold (1910–1997), Betty R. Rebold-Henry (1915–2003), and Mary Belle June Rebold-Lasher (1926–2014).

Alice Emma Rebold also remained in Bridgeburg.

Alice Emma Rebold.

Catherine "Katie" (1886–1978) married Ralph Robert Gray (1886–1930) on March 8, 1911, and remained in Bridgeburg. Their children were Julia Belle Gray-Boyd, Cecil Warren Gray, Marguerite Gray, and John, Robert, and Paul Gray.

John H. Rebold was known for his building of the Bridge View Hotel in Mosgrove. Many famous people stayed at the Bridge View, such as William Jennings Bryan. He also built the Bridgeburg Brickyard, which later was known as Haws Refractories. A fire destroyed the Bridge View in 1914. Later, my aunt Sadie Whited-Cloak took over the building, and it again became a hotel while renting boats out as well.

(See a photo of the Bridge View Hotel on the following page.)

Shown is the Bridge View Hotel and the railroad bridge. Could that be Boss Patton in the boat?

Builder's Grandson Recalls...
Mosgrove's Bridge View Hotel Once Tourist Mecca

"The well-known Bridge View Hotel caught fire this afternoon, and at 3 o'clock the roof was in flames."

So read the Kittanning Daily Leader edition of Nov. 4, 1914, the day when one of the upper Allegheny's foremost tourist attractions disappeared in flames, never to be replaced.

The Bridge View Hotel with its 45 rooms and a bar attracted tourists from Pittsburgh who made the trip on the Pennsylvania Railroad for a quiet vacation on the river.

Notable among the return visitors was the famous orator and presidential candidate William Jennings Bryan who stayed at the Bridge View several times. Bryan claimed, according to A. L. Heinrich, grandson of the hotel's builder, that he got more rest there than anywhere in the country.

"Bryan always wanted the corner room on Pine Creek," Heinrich remembers. "There was a Hemlock tree near the window, and he liked the scent of hemlock and the breeze from the creek."

Heinrich's grandfather John Rebold built the hotel in 1901, and his father William A. Heinrich operated it for his brother-in-law for about four years. Rebold at that time moved to Oklahoma where he later acquired a fortune in oil drilling.

Pittsburgh Plate Glass Co. at that time had a coal mine at Mosgrove, supplying the Ford City plant with fuel for power generating. When PPG began buying power from West Penn Power Co. about 1913 the mine closed.

Heinrich recalls that the bar business must have been the mainstay of the hotel, because business slackened greatly after the miners moved from the area.

Vacationers from Pittsburgh continued to patronize the Bridge View, and the hotel owned a 30-passenger boat which was used to transport fishermen and picnickers to an island which lay near the present location of Dam 8.

Rebold's son Grant took charge of the hotel during its last years while his father was building a brick yard at West Mosgrove.

The Daily Leader the day following the fire in 1914 said the blaze lasted only 1½ hours, consuming the structure.

"Damage was estimated at $25,000," the newspaper account said, "of which only $15,000 was covered by insurance."

The flames, attributed to a defective flue, endangered nearby homes and burned ¼-mile up Pine Creek.

Ironically, the next day's edition of the Daily Leader carried an account of the old McKee place, a former hotel at Cowansville, also burning to the ground.

Increasing efforts are being made today in Armstrong County to attract tourists and recreationists to the waters of the upper Allegheny. Only a few people, however, remember the days when the Bridge View Hotel made its significant contribution to the area's economy through tourism.

Oilman, Lumberman, Hotel Operator...

Mosgrove Native Death Ends Storybook Career

A famed native of Mosgrove, John H. Rebold, died Thursday in Oklahoma, ending an almost storybook life as pioneer oilman, lumberman and hotelman.

Rebold, 94, reportedly made three fortunes in his lifetime. He knew many famous men personally, including Presidents Woodrow Wilson and Herbert Hoover, William Jennings Bryan, Andrew Carnegie, Charles Schwab and W. G. McAdoo.

Born Sept. 2, 1872 in Mosgrove, he was a son of Mr. and Mrs. Henry Rebold. He died at 6 p.m. Thursday, Nov. 30, in a hospital in Okmulgee, Okla., after being taken ill at Rebold Manor Rest Home, Okmulgee.

A drilling contractor in Kittanning for many years, Rebold was the founder of the Bridgeburg brick works, now operated as a unit of Haws Refractories Co. He also built Bridge View Hotel, a once famous resort hotel at Mosgrove, since destroyed by fire.

In 1906 he went to Okmulgee in search of oil and there brought in his first Oklahoma well in 1909, the first of many. He built the Tiger Refinery, later to become the Barnsdall Refinery, in association with his old boss and friend Theodore Barnsdall, head of an oil empire.

In early 1914 Rebold began building Rebold Mansion in Okmulgee at a cost of $150,000. Architect was the famed Horace LaPierre. The result was a fabulous 17-room showplace which attracted visitors from all over the country.

The inside was paneled throughout in solid walnut, and had handpainted ceiling murals, handpainted tapestries on the walls, imported rugs and crystal chandeliers hanging in

(See 2 on Page Two)

On Inside Pages

Amusement	17
Classified Ads	18-19
Comics	16
Deaths	19
Editorial	6
Financial	5
Ford City	4
Religious News	8
Sports	14-15
Women's Pages	10-11

Now Those Russians Think They Can Regulate Love

MOSCOW (UPI)—Love in a spaceship is a necessity and Russia must officially recognize it, a Soviet scientist said today.

Igor Zabelin warned "Love as an emotion will play a very important role in the future in the populating of outer space. We must not only deeper analyze love as an emotion but also try to regulate it properly."

Writing in the magazine "Moskva" Zabelin predicted "In th efuture, when mankind will fulfill its mission of populating outer space, men and women will be sent in spacecraft somewhere for many years."

Noting that "when a couple lives together for five to seven years, they may get sick of each other and very often there is a divorce," Zabelin warned such coolness could cause grave problems in outer space.

"The factor of love must be taken into special consideration because it will serve an important role in their life in outer space," he said of future space colonizers.

"Love has a cosmic factor," he said. "It is very important and we must pay far more attention to this problem than we do now."

Today's Chuckle

As Confucius said: "The price of success is readily worked out in the income tax tables."
(Copr. T-M, 1966 Gen. Fea. Corp.)

Continued from Page One

all the downstairs rooms.

The mansion was razed in 1962 and a modern 84-bed nursing home, Rebold Manor, in which Rebold was living at the time of his death, was constructed on its site.

Rebold made several return trips to his home state, Pennsylvania. After retiring, he drilled the first deep wildcat well in the northeastern part of the state, near Scranton. He later returned to Okmulgee and decided to spend the rest of his life doing things he had never had time for before, such as hunting and fishing.

However, shortly before his 94th birthday, he wrote his nephew, Albert Heinrich of Adrian, that he was preparing to drill his 1,004th oil well.

"He saw the oil industry progress from the days of wooden pipe to 36-inch steel lines laid from the Gulf of New York and Philadelphia," Heinrich said. "When he started out, you couldn't give gasoline away— there were no autos then. Now we have jet planes and flying astronauts."

Rebold's first wife and mother of his children, the former Laura Cornman of Mosgrove, died in 1910.

He is survived by four sons: Grant of Okmulgee, Jesse J. of Houston, Texas, Joseph of Udall, Kansas and Harry of Tulsa, Okla.; a daughter: Katherine Rebold of Tulsa, Okla.; one brother: George of Cowansville; one sister: Mrs. Robert (Katherine) Gray of Rochester, Pa.; 14 grandchildren and numerous great-grandchildren. One son, Brian, and one daughter, Julie Ann, preceded him in death.

Henry H. Johns Family

Henry "Heenie" Harrison Johns (1878–1944) married Nannie Elen Flenner-Johns (1879–1948). Their children were Hollis B. Johns (1901–1975), James Henry Johns (1903–1957), Garnet Catherine Johns-Slagle (1904–1992), Ailene Caroline Johns-Johns (1906–1995), Clifford "Fish" Roger Johns (1908–1972), Arnold "Quig" Johns (1910–date of death not known), Wilson "Doe" Johns (1912–1950), Wilfred Earl Johns (1912–1974), Martha Elizabeth Johns (1914–1914), Vernon Benjamin Johns (1918–1976), Clarence Eugene Johns (1920–1989), and Charles R. Johns (1921–2000).

Wilson and Wilfred were twins. Wilson was killed in a tragic railroad accident in 1950. Clarence and James were good friends to all of us kids growing up. Clarence had a sense of humor out of this world. Jim had much determination in life as he lived with an artificial leg and was able to work at Haws Refractories for many years. Clarence and James remained in Bridgeburg. Clarence married later in life.

Clifford "Fish" R. Johns remained in Bridgeburg for many years on the Smokey Cousins Farm. He married Harriet C. Johns (1908–2000). Their children were Samuel, Richard, Norma, Nancy, Martha, Andrew, and Ruth.

Henry Johns' home as it is today.

William Mateer Family

William Mateer was born in 1840. In 1870 he married Sarah Jane Helm. In 1884, they bought a sixty-acre farm in West Mosgrove/Bridgeburg. Two of their ten children were born there. Their children were Sharon Mateer, Lola Mateer, Julia Belle Mateer, Elizabeth Ethel Mateer-Rockwell, Ida May Mateer, Charles Helms Mateer, Edith Wilhelmina Mateer-Wylie, Ora Mabel Mateer-Wolff, George Kay Mateer, and Jay E. Mateer (1890–1959), who attended the Myers School.

Jay was very popular in Bridgeburg as he was the telegrapher for the BR&P Railroad, which later became the B&O Railroad. Jay had many duties at the station, including passing messages to passing trains via a long pole with the messages attached. As the train passed by, Jay held out the pole with the message, and the trainman would reach out and grab the message from the pole. As kids, we used to loaf at the West Mosgrove Station and watch Jay do his work as a telegrapher. Jay later built his home on the original sixty-acre farm.

The home that Jay Mateer was raised in later became property of Haws Refractories. After the Mateer family left the farm when we were kids, Frank and Mert Hiwiller lived there. After the Hiwillers left and Haws Refractories owned the house, it stood wide-open. As kids, we used to play there using it as our fort during snowball fights. The building no longer remains. The old stone barn from the farm casually remains.

Jay E. Mateer first married Ida Irene Milliron-Mateer (1888–1915), and they had a son, Frederick (1914–1959). Jay later married Emma Edna McAuley-Mateer (1895–1990). Their children were Muriel M. Mateer-Beckett (1921–2007), Thomas W. Mateer (1923–1974), and Raymond J. Mateer (1925–2010).

Original Mateer farm.

Rear view of the Jay Mateer home today.

Mateer stone barn as it is today.

Freeman Family

Robert Clark "Nappy" Freeman was born on February 6, 1879, and passed on January 25, 1957. His parents were James L. Freeman (1850–1932) and Sarah Hockenberry-Freeman (1853–1903).

Robert Clark was born in Madison, Clarion County, Pennsylvania. He married Sarah Ann "Sadie" Swigart-Freeman (1882–1977). They settled in an area of Bridgeburg referred to as the Heckle Place, far south in Bridgeburg. Their children were John James Freeman (1900–1974), Harry Opal Freeman (1902–2002), Charles Kenneth "Red" Freeman (1905–1981), Minnie Freeman-Cobbett (1907–1978), Clarence "Baldy" Freeman (1910–2002), Clark E. "Mutt" Freeman (1913–1994), and William Freeman (?–2002).

Clark "Mutt" Freeman remained in Bridgeburg. He married Laura Ruby Hooks-Freeman. They had two children: Robert E. Freeman and Ronald L. Freeman.

Robert Clark "Nappy" Freeman.

Robert Clark Freeman (left) and other person not identified.

Clair Cloak and Kenneth "Red" Freeman.

William Freeman.

Clark "Mutt" Freeman holding Carla Whited.

Laura Ruby Hooks-Freeman.

Robert Freeman.

Ronald Freeman.

Debbie Freeman-Sanders, daughter of Ronald and Sandy Greenawalt-Freeman

Schaub Family

Charles John Schaub (1843–1911) was married to Susan Friday-Schaub. Their son, Edward Lewis Schaub (1877–1961), married Jeanette "Nettie" Swigart-Schaub (1880–1964). Their children were Clarence Schaub (1899–1985), Hazel Melinda Schaub-Johnston (1903–1981), Lewis Edward Schaub (1904–1985), Theodore Arthur Schaub (1906–1987), William Herbert Schaub (1908–1983), Lawrence F. Schaub (1911–1996), Elmer Schaub (1914–1995), Raymond Vernon Schaub (1917–1998), Fred N. Schaub (1923–1999), and Thomas Schaub (?–1981)

(Left–right) Clarence Schaub, Simon Cousins, and Spuc Cousins.

Hazel Schaub married George Johnston and remained in the Bridgeburg area. Their children were Arlie, Paul, Ruth, Catherine, and Judith.

Judith Johnston.

The Schaub farm was located on the top of Quigley Hill across the cemetery. Their son, Lewis, peddled vegetables from their garden to all Bridgeburg residents. In addition to the vegetables, he also included fresh chickens that was still alive. I remember my mother chopping the heads off the giant Rhode Island Red roosters. Those roosters made for a very delicious meal! Lewis also peddled eggs and many other items.

Lawrence "Horn" F. Schaub remained in Bridgeburg and married Margaret Ellen Croyle-Schaub. Their children were Vera Jean, June, and Avanell.

Fred N. Schaub remained in Bridgeburg for many years and married Gladys Aldean-Schaub. They had a daughter, Freda Schaub-Peters.

Clarence B. Swigart Family

Clarence B. Swigart, (03-19-1857 to 02-11-1946) married Malinda Swigart (1865–1933). Their children were Sarah "Sadie" Ann Swigart-Freeman, Nettie Swigart-Schaub, and Jesse Swigart.

John K. Tarr Family

John Kirk Tarr (1844–1923) married Martha Jane Myers-Tarr (1844–1929). Their children were Mrs. WH Moore of Mosgrove, mother of Belva Moore-Painter, who was our close neighbor; Lossie Tarr-Bryson (1869–1951) of Ford City, Pennsylvania; Jacob Tarr (1871–1936) of East Franklin Township; Joseph Tarr (1875–1944) of Derry, Pennsylvania; Mrs. Charles Montgomery (1874–1955) of Tarrtown; Mrs. JA Zellefrow of Newark, Ohio; David Tarr (1881–1962) of West Kittanning; John Tarr of Detroit, Michigan; and Robert L. Tarr (1888–1971).

(Left–right) Orie Patton, Jacob Tarr, and unidentified person.

Original John and Martha Tarr home.

Robert Tarr Family

Robert Tarr (1888–1971) stayed and worked on their farm in Bridgeburg. He married Olive Stiveson-Tarr. Their children were Pearl, Clarence "Mouse," Mildred, Delbert "Delp," Leslie "Blain", Gertrude, Harry, Betty, and Belva June.

I never will forget Delp Tarr. He used to fish with us when we were kids. He plowed all our gardens with his trusty horses, Bill and Roy. Their farm was nestled on the Quigley Hill Road.

Joseph Steffey Family

Joseph M. Steffey married Margaret Rebold-Steffey on May 27, 1902. Their children were Margaret Bell Steffey-Emelton, Walter "Wick" Steffey, Chester "Ted" Steffey, George H. "Hen" Steffey, Gene Steffey, and Bernice Steffey-Patton. Their home was situated on the Rebold farm road.

Gene Steffey was killed in action during World War II. Joseph Steffey was a big part of the Bridgeburg Sunday school.

Walter Steffey (1904–1972) remained in Bridgeburg for several years. He married Minnie Ritchey-Steffey. They had one son, Wilford "Booge" Steffey. In the 1950s, Wick and Minnie owned a small store on the River Road near their home. He was also employed at Haws Refractories

Chester "Ted" Steffey (1908–1979) remained in Bridgeburg. He married Alice Fink-Steffey. Their children were Chester "Junior" Steffey Jr. and Jack Steffey. He, too, worked at Haws Refractories.

Junior Steffey married Shirley Gray-Steffey, and they had four children. Jack Steffey married Myrna Barnhart-Steffey, and they also had four children.

I will never forget Hen Steffey at our Sunday school. He used to bring in religious records and play them for us. One record he played often was "It Is No Secret (What God Can Do)."

Chester "Junior" Steffey.

Jack Steffey.

Haines Zellefrow Family

Haines Zellefrow was born on August 5, 1866, and passed away on June 4, 1952. His spouse was Malissa Bowser-Zellefrow (06-14-1863 to 10-12-1952). They married in 1888. Their children were Grant D. Zellefrow, Ford L. Zellefrow, Ada Francis Zellefrow, and Daniel Zellefrow. Haines was a farmer who resided on the Quigley Hill Road.

Dan Zellefrow, shall we say, was a wanna-be replica of the Wild West as he touted his six guns. While extremely high on cheap wine, Dan shot at anything, and I mean *anything*!

A story I would never forget was when one day Dan asked Bud Boring if he would take Dan to Kittanning to buy his groceries. Bud said that he would take him, but only if Dan left his guns at home. "I promise, Bud!" So off to Kittanning they went. Dan bought his groceries, and then on their way home, somewhere near the #7 Lock, Dan drew his gun which was hidden in his jacket and proclaimed, "I lied to you, Bud!" Dan then wound down the window on Bud's 1936 Oldsmobile. His target was the car's hood ornament. He shot at it, but I can't recall whether he hit the hood ornament or not. Bud was in deep fear as he proclaimed that the percussion alone scared him half to death. This is just one of the many stories about Dan Zellefrow and his shooting escapades.

Peter Tatsak Family

Peter John Tatsak was born on June 15, 1889, in Slovakia and passed away in 1970. He married Anna Kuchera on June 17, 1911. Peter worked on the B&O Railroad as a repair foreman. Their residence was a B&O company house located just before the bridge in Bridgeburg. They had three sons—William, Thomas John, and Jack—and seven daughters—Ann Tatsak-Moore, Helen Tatsak-Lukach, Mary Tatsak-Leitgeb, Margaret Tatsak-Lockhart, Olga Tatsak-Clark, Irene Tatsak-Bieniek, and Nancy Tatsak-Wyant.

When the Peter Tatsak family left Bridgeburg and moved to West Kittanning in the early 1950s, the Lewis Johns family moved into their house and lived there for several years.

Thomas John Tatsak.

Lewis Johns Family

Lewis Johns was born on August 11, 1905, and passed away on August 30, 1960. His spouse was Emily Cochran-Johns. Their children were Samantha and Erma Johns. Lewis was employed at Haws Refractories.

(Back) Lewis and Emily Johns and
(front) daughters Erma and Samantha.

Erma Johns-Lowman and Samantha Johns at home (former home of the Peter Tatsak family), July 1954.

Fred Cousins Family

Fred Cousins was born in 1881 and married Martha "Matt" Ruffner-Cousins, born in 1891. Their children were Frank Hockenberry (adopted), born in 1904, and Thomas Cousins (03-05-1918 to 03-05-1989). Tom married Constance B. Zellefrow-Cousins (06-13-1919 to 11-14-1996), and they had two children.

Lebbeous Cousins Family

Lebbeous "Leb" cousins (1874–1942) married Sarah Jane Cousins. Their children were Gretta Frances Cousins-Toy, Alma Lupa Cousins-Zellefrow, and Pluma Dakota Cousins-Duncan.

Leb Cousins and Wes Whited.

Gretta Cousins.

Alma Cousins.

Andrew Ruffner Family

Andrew Ruffner was born in 1855 and passed on April 10, 1939. His spouse was Sarah Ellen Ruffner. Their children were Martha Margaret Ruffner-Cousins, Sarah Jane Ruffner-Cousins, and Ella Mae Ruffner-Claypoole.

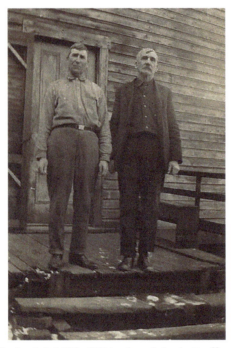

(Left–right) Wes Whited and Andy Ruffner.

William Albert Heinrich Family

William Albert Heinrich (1875–1944) married Julia Ann Rebold-Heinrich (1876–1962). Their son was Albert Leslie "Bricky" Heinrich (1901–1977), who married Mary Elizabeth Schnitzler-Heinrich (1910–1993). Their children were Albert Leslie (1942–), William, and Marlene.

Robert Cowan Family

Robert G. Cowan was born on September 28, 1891, and passed away on April 5, 1952. He married Elvira Alberta McCauley-Cowan (10-02-1892 to 12-27-1977). They had one daughter, Ruth Cowan.

Arthur Luke Family

Arthur Luke (09-07-1904 to 01-25-1990) married Velma Margaret "Dot" Farester-Luke (11-14-1910 to 10-27-2010). They had a daughter, Marlene Luke-Chasse, who married Lionel "Leo" Chasse. Their children were Doug and Debbie. Doug was very helpful with his contributions to this writing.

Clarence Boring Family

Clarence "Bud" Boring (01-24-1918 to 02-05-2008) married Mary Grace Forsythe-Boring (02-28-1920 to 10-11-2011). Their children were Mitzie (1940–1955), Daniel (1941–), who was my age, and Susan Boring-Steffey (1962–).

The Clarence "Bud" Boring family was from Bolivar, Pennsylvania. Bud worked at the brickyard and previously lived in the old Mateer house that was presently occupied by Frank and Mert Hiwiller. The Boring family eventually moved into the row house next to our home. Bud, as a youngster, contracted polio and walked with crutches, but was so determined to live life just as anyone else, and he did so admirably. Mitzie passed away at age fifteen in 1955 because of leukemia. It was an incredibly sad moment for this family and for all of us. Growing up, she was our pal.

Clarence "Bud" Boring.

Mary Boring.

Mitzie Boring's obituary.

Dan Boring and his mother, Mary Boring.

(Left–right) Ellen Lash and Mitzie Boring on the railroad bridge.

Mitzie Boring.

Dan Boring.

Susan Boring-Steffey.

Frank Cloak Family

Frank Cloak (1909–1986) married Gertrude E. Whited-Cloak (1903–1989) Frank was employed at Haws Refractories. They had one son, Jack N. Cloak (07-20-1931 to 10-23-2004). Jack married Etta Croyle-Cloak on May 14, 1960. They had four children.

GOING OVERSEAS

PVT. JACK M. CLOAK is at Camp Stoneman, Calif., awaiting assignment to duties in the Far East. A son of Mr. and Mrs. Frank Cloak of Bridgeburg, the infantryman entered military service November 18, 1952. He trained with the Fifth Infantry Division at Indiantown Gap, before he was sent to Camp Stoneman on March 27. (Baney photo)

Jack Cloak.

Jack and Etta Croyle-Cloak's wedding (05-14-1960).

John S. Painter Family

John S. Painter (06-07-1900 to 12-23-1961) married Belva Moore-Painter (07-03-1903 to 12-31-1982). Their children were Homer J. Painter and George W. Painter.

George Painter (05-25-1922 to 03-07-1984) married Mildred "Honey" Rumbarger-Painter. They had five children.

Homer J. Painter (09-30-1924 to 10-18-1994) married Avanell Lasher-Painter on September 14, 1946. They had five children.

Homer J. Painter.

Frank L. Hockenberry Sr. Family

Frank L. Hockenberry Sr. (09-24-1904 to 11-06-1985) married Mabern Wolff-Hockenberry (11-07-1907 to 08-28-1986). Their children were Winifred Hockenberry-Weaver, Joanne Hockenberry-Hooks, Jay D. Hockenberry, Frank L. Hockenberry Jr., and Eddie Joe Hockenberry.

Eddie Joe Hockenberry.

Frank Hockenberry Jr.

Frank Hockenberry Sr.

Raymond G. Wolfe Family

Raymond G Wolfe, born on October 7, 1926, (as of this writing) still resides in Bridgeburg. He married Phyllis A. Wagner-Wolfe (1928–2010). They had four children.

Chamie Hooks Family

Chamie Hooks was born on March 15, 1925 and passed away on January 16, 2015. His spouse was Patricia Futscher-Hooks. Their children were Chamie, Deborah, and Brenda Hooks. Chamie was one of Armstrong County's best baseball players!

Simon E. Anderson Family

Simon E. "Gene" Anderson (1914–) married Josephine Mae Atherton-Anderson (September 4, 1914 to August 20, 1964). Their children were Jane, Incel E. "Bud," and James.

Thomas Crowe Family

Thomas Crowe (06-09-1915 to 10-20-2002) married Jenny E. Croyle-Crowe (07-13-1916 to 01-16-2008). Their children were Richard T. Crowe, Keith H. Crowe, Enos A. Crowe, and Daniel Crowe.

Richard Crowe was killed in an automobile accident in 1951.

Harold Walker Family

Harold Walker (1920–1977) married Martha L. Walker (1923–1999). Their children were Rose, Betty, Harold "Butch," James, Joanne, and Sandra.

Rose Walker.

Frank Hiwiller Family

Frank Hiwiller (04-09-1896 to 11-1970). He married Margaret Viola Heller-Hiwiller (1903–1944). They had three daughters.

He then married Myrtle Bell Redick-Hiwiller (1911–1963).

CHAPTER 4

The Railroads

The railroads were a very significant part of Bridgeburg, with three major railroads meandering across and through this tiny community. They were the BR&P (Buffalo, Rochester, and Pittsburgh), later to become the B&O (Baltimore and Ohio), the Shawmut Railroad, and directly across the river in Mosgrove was the Pennsylvania Railroad. The Pennsylvania Railroad, or the Pennsy as it was called, was not directly located in Bridgeburg, but served as a transfer for those residents of Bridgeburg for transportation into Kittanning. They simply had to walk across the bridge to acquire a ride on "The Pennsy" to Kittanning and beyond.

The BR&P Railroad

By the middle of the nineteenth century, American industry had finally found the means of transporting bituminous coal from Western Pennsylvania by transporting it straight from the mines to those who needed it. That means was for a railroad to haul the coal from the hills of Pennsylvania to Rochester and Buffalo, New York, and many other towns and locales in between to satisfy those needs. Thus, the BR&P Railroad was formed.

It seems by 1880, the United States had 17,800 freight locomotives carrying approximately 23,600 tons of freight and 22,200 passengers and was, indeed, the largest employer in the country. The BR&P established itself as a coal hauler in the early days and, by the 1880s, had proven itself as a major coal hauler to many much-needed areas. In order to meet demands for "King Coal," many bridges had to be built. By the 1890s, passenger service also was available. Thus, the bridge at West Mosgrove, later Bridgeburg, just had to be built across the Allegheny River. This bridge, after many laborious hours and the use of many laborers, was completed in 1899, assuring that coal and passengers could be safely delivered on time to many more places.

Total length of the bridge is 1,682 feet with a height of 110 feet. It is officially named Baltimore Deck Truss Bridge over Allegheny River on BR&P Railroad. This bridge was decked with safety rails on both sides. With the completion of this new bridge, it was quite appropriate to rename this small village Bridgeburg although the railroad station was still referred to as the West Mosgrove Station.

Joyce Toussaint-Whited at the West Mosgrove Station, July 1967.

West Mosgrove Station, March 1955.

It is said that Sarah Ann "Sadie" Swigart-Freeman was the first to walk across the bridge after its completion. Supposedly, the bridge still remains in use today. During World War I, the bridge was guarded by military guards and, during World War II, by nonmilitary, security guards to prevent possible sabotage.

The completed Baltimore Deck Truss Bridge Over Allegheny River on BR&P Railroad.

The railroad bridge, November 2019.

There was a watering tank located just before the bridge, close to the station, for use by the early locomotive steam engines that had to have water to produce the steam power. There was a pump house close to the river near the bridge that pumped water from the river up the long hill to the watering tank. This pump house was fueled by coal that was lowered down to the pump house from the bridge (according to former residents Jack Steffey and Tom McAfoose). Arthur Luke was the pump-house operator for many years. He also was the community barber, and as kids, we got our haircuts in the pump house for twenty-five cents. After the pump house was gone, he used his home basement as his barbershop.

The BR&P remained until 1932 when the B&O took over the lines. The pump house and the water tank remained until the early 1950s when steam locomotives were eased out because of the coming of diesel engines.

Tom Mix, the very famous Western cowboy hero in the early days of (silent) movie making, was originally from Mix Run in Elk County in Pennsylvania. He sometimes took the train from Hollywood to his hometown in Pennsylvania. Airlines were still unavailable in those days. When he came as far as the West Mosgrove station on the BR&P, he had to transfer to the Pennsylvania Railroad by walking the bridge to Mosgrove to catch his train to Mix Run. Now, naturally, he needed help in carrying his baggage across the bridge. All the young boys were quite aware of their hero passing through, and all volunteered to carry his baggage, for they knew that a huge tip was in store.

Tom Mix, Hollywood's first mega Western movie star.

My dad was the smallest of the group and seemed to be pushed aside by the older and bigger boys. Mix recognized this and chose my dad to carry his baggage across the bridge. Dad told me this story many times.

It was always a thrill to be walking across the bridge when, suddenly, as you might be halfway across, a train came on the bridge! You had the deck and guardrails, and you simply held on until the train passed. Several times we were caught on the bridge while going trout fishing in Pine Creek. We usually went fishing early in the morning with Laverne Wolfe and Bob Freeman. It was hard to just stand there and hold on while also holding on to our fishing gear!

The Pittsburgh and Shawmut Railroad

The Pittsburgh and Shawmut engine (photo by Randy Kiser).

The Pittsburgh and Shawmut Railroad was a big part of my life as our home was located just some four hundred feet east of the rail line in Bridgeburg. Coal was the principal commodity for delivery for the rail line's whole existence. Planning for construction of the lines began in 1903, and the actual construction began in 1906.

As rumors were told of the new rail line, it was noted that the Patton family in Bridgeburg disagreed heartily with the new railroad cutting through their property and fought it heatedly. The railroad finally won out, but the Patton family still disagreed.

Although as mentioned before, coal was the principal commodity, other industries were included like the Haws Refractories in Bridgeburg. Haws eventually made the type of products used in the steel industry and were also used later in the war effort in World War II and beyond. The railroad had what was called a spur that connected the Shawmut with the B&O at Bridgeburg. Thus, the products from Haws eventually were delivered by means of the B&O Railroad to many ports of destination. Other industries using the Pittsburgh and Shawmut rails included a lumberyard and the Linde Air Company in Kittanning that shipped their industrial gases using the Shawmut rails.

There was also another passageway to the BR&P and later the B&O from the Shawmut at Bridgeburg and was referred to as the Great Elevator. This was no more than a cut-in road extending on the west side of the hill in Bridgeburg up to near the West Mosgrove station. The road started close to my aunt Edna Hook's residence. Evidently, this was before the railroad spur.

As a youngster, when the train rolled through during the day on the Shawmut, all of us kids would wait as the brakemen and signalmen used to ride the caboose on the train. Jim Bennet from Brookville used to throw candy off to us kids from his perch in the caboose. Jim was a family friend. His wife, Lydia, was a sister of my aunt Audrey Dolby-Whited. Years later, Dan Boring and I were invited to ride in the caboose onto the spur to the B&O by brakeman Paul Dunn.

Shawmut Railroad passenger train as seen from our front yard (June 1955).

CHAPTER 5

Coming of Locks on the River

It was probably in the early 1920s that the plan went into effect for building locks or dams on the Allegheny River. There were nine altogether built between the middle 1920s and early 1930s. The reasoning, of course, was for better navigation and recreational purposes. The dam closest to Bridgeburg was Lock #8 closer to Reesedale. Lock #7 was located down the Alleghany River in Kittanning.

Lock #8 has been referred to as a historic lock and fixed-crest dam complex located at Boggs and Washington townships in Armstrong County. It was built between 1929 and 1931 by the United States Army Corps of Engineers and consists of the lock, dam, esplanade, and operations building. The lock measures 56 feet by 360 feet and has a lift of 17.8 feet. The dam measures approximately 56 feet high and 916 feet long; a 3-foot addition was built on top of the dam in 1937. This was part of an extensive system of locks and dams as previously said to improve navigation along the Allegheny River. There were many Bridgeburg residents who were employed in building this dam.

Lock #8 on the Allegheny River, close to Bridgeburg.

Shawmut Lines Hoodlebug

The Hoodlebug was a name used for a small gasoline-powered motorcar on the Shawmut used for commuter purposes. That was when there were no buses and only a few cars. It provided transportation in rural areas for those between towns or cities to factories and other municipalities. It also provided service for students going to or from school. I know some of my cousins used the Hoodlebug to go to Kittanning High School from Bridgeburg and return home after school. The cost was a bare minimum. It was discontinued in the late 1930s as buses and automobiles came into the forefront.

The students from both points north and south of Kittanning were unable to reach classes for one day because fire had damaged both motorized coaches. The blaze broke out from some undetermined cause in one of the passenger coaches housed in a steel building at Timblin.

On January 9, 1935, an estimated one hundred Kittanning High School students who reached school each day via the Pittsburgh and Shawmut passenger car (Hoodlebug) had near-normal service restored to them when a passenger coach and steam locomotive replaced two gasoline-powered passenger coaches that were heavily damaged by fire.

There was also a Shawmut train station in Bridgeburg that was located close to the Bridgeburg store, in between the main railroad and the spur to Haws Refractories.

Shawmut Lines Hoodlebug in the 1920s
(Photo credit to Walter J. Hill
from Pittsburg, Shawmut, and Northern by Paul Pietrak).

CHAPTER 6

My Remembrances

I can actually say that I was born under a bridge, the Bridgeburg Bridge! I came into this world on August 14, 1941, in the northernmost Patton house that was located just a little south of this great bridge. Dr. Joseph Milliron of Kittanning delivered me, but had a hard time taking the rocky path down from the top river road and only had my father's guidance with a flashlight. Years later, he told me that he tripped over the rocks and received cuts and bruises before reaching his final destination to deliver me into this cruel world. Thank you, Dr. Milliron! I had an older brother, Larry, who was two weeks shy of being exactly two years older than me. My father was Elvin Otto "Webb" Whited, and my mother was Winifred Madge Moors-Whited, from Leesburg or the Mercer, Pennsylvania, area.

My uncle Carl Whited (my dad's brother) and his wife, Aunt Catherine "Cass," lived in the larger Patton house that was close to the house in which I was born. Aunt Cass, my uncle Carl, and their family consisted of daughters Betty and Doris and a son, William "Bud," who was killed in an auto accident in 1947.

I believe we moved southward in 1943 to one of the row houses that were company houses for Haws Refractories. Ours was the second house to the right, looking toward the Shawmut Railroad. Clark "Mutt" Freeman and his wife, Ruby Hooks-Freeman (a daughter of my aunt Edna), and sons, Robert and Ronald, lived in the first house. Ed and Lil Wyant and Lil's daughter, Imogene Wasson, lived in the third house. Frank and Gertrude Whited-Cloak and son, Jack, lived in the fourth house, and John and Belva Moore-Painter and sons, George and Homer, lived in the fifth house. They were comfy small, two-bedroom bungalow homes built right on the riverbank, which afforded a view of the river that was absolutely beautiful! All those who lived there were employees of Haws Refractories. My father and mother lived there until 1983.

Far right house was where I was born. Far left house was where Uncle Carl Whited and his family lived.

Far left house from above photo as it is today after a huge tree fell through the roof of the house.

Bridgeburg General Store

The store was located close to the Shawmut, with a small road on the west side that crossed over the railroad track and served as an entrance to the brickyard. The road continued past the brickyard, giving both an exit and entrance to the River Road for those who lived in the row houses, who had driveways connected to this little access road.

There are many stories connected to this store building that was very convenient for buying groceries, meats, and most everything else including ice cream, pop, and candy treats at prices that are hard to believe in this modern age.

I can remember very well that both Mont and Boss Patton rowed their boats down to buy their groceries at the store. They tied their boats to our old oak tree.

The store, as I recall, was managed by Ed and Lil Wyant when we arrived in the row houses. Later it was managed by Elmer and Ida Zimmerman, and by 1947 it was owned and operated by the Frank Hockenberry family who lived in the store building.

Frank also worked at the brickyard. Their daughter Winifred Hockenberry-Weaver and her family also had a small apartment in the building. The Hockenberry family also included wife, Mabern, and sons, Jay, Frank Jr., and Eddie Joe. Another daughter, Joann, later moved into the building. All the young Bridgeburg kids hung out at this store, and some romances started there as well. Some of those youths included Jack and Junior Steffey, Jack Hooks, Tom and Jack Tatsak, Jack Cloak, Gerald Wise, Jim Rebold, Bob and Merle Gray, Jay Hockenberry, Booge Steffey, Charlie and Bob Johns, and Homer and George Painter.

At one point, the Hockenberrys installed a billiard parlor in the main part of the store (petitioned off from the regular store), which attracted adult menfolk from far and wide. As young kids, we were all in awe just watching the different people entering this pool hall. People came from miles around, some who appeared to come from a little higher social status than we were used to as was evidenced by their cars.

Mabern Hockenberry also cooked lunch specials mostly for the brickyard workers, giving them a good lunch for a good price within the store. It was probably 1946 or earlier when the Ed Wyant family moved into the store building and left the row house next to us open. I believe Imogene Wasson, who was Lil's daughter, lived there for a while.

Imogene Wasson.

At the young age of four, I remember VJ Day as war with Japan had finally ended. The reason I remember this so well is that the siren at the brickyard blew all day long. Plus, it was my birthday!

The Hooks family also lived in the store building early on. It consisted of the mother, Mary, and sons, Walt, Ivan, and Merle.

Due to the war effort, there were some ladies who worked at the brickyard. Those that I remember were my aunt Sadie Whited-Cloak, Evie Ambrose, Ida Lasher, and Aidah Hepfl. This was hard work for those ladies, and they did a great job!

At age six, in September 1947, I marched off to the first grade at the one-room Bridgeburg schoolhouse that was just a few hundred feet from our residence, located on the west side of the River Road. This one-room school consisted of all eight grades. The teacher was Mabel Henry, who could be very mean and expected everyone to learn. My first-grade class consisted of Martha Johns, Lloyd Myers, Danny Boring, and myself. As I recall, the school consisted of some forty students in eight grades.

Just a little bit south of the schoolhouse was the residence of my grandfather John Wesley "Pap" Whited. My aunts Hazel and Nora also resided there. My grandmother Laura Jane Patton-Whited passed away in 1913 when my father was only three years old.

Aunt Hazel was a sight to behold! She was a big part of my early life as a babysitter and as a favorite aunt. She was very good-looking, gracious, and high-strung, very friendly, and very likable and always willing to help in all family needs. She could make you laugh in an instant. She had a nickname for everyone she knew.

She never married but devoted her life to caring for her father.

My aunt Nora was divorced and moved in with my grandfather and Aunt Hazel.

Bridgeburg School

On the outside, the school was topped with a steeple and a giant bell that rang accordingly for recess and the beginning of classes. On the inside was a little hallway where the rope to toll the bell was placed. As you entered the classroom, off to the left was a big blackboard with the ABCs on top, a large portrait of George Washington, and close to fifty desks with inkwells. A piano also fitted in nicely in the northwest corner of the room. On the northeast side was our library of books and encyclopedias. Those encyclopedias were purchased with money raised from a cakewalk that brought many residents to the event, including auctioneer Frank Heinen, who auctioned off many cakes and pastries.

Heating was provided at first by a large coal furnace that sat on the southwest part of the room. A few years later the coal furnace was replaced by a potbellied stove. A student monitor was chosen by the teacher to start the fires in the morning and keep the room warm all day. Richard Johns was the monitor when I arrived for school. Later, Bob Freeman was chosen, and later Charles Zimmerman was given the duties.

There was no running water or restrooms, only outhouses. Our water was supplied by carrying buckets of water from Belva and John Painter's home and put in a crocklike tank with a spigot. We had to supply our own drinking cups. Again, those who carried the water were chosen by the teacher. Sometimes while carrying water, Belva would give us treats. Nothing was more delicious than her famous cherry dream cake!

Recess was two fifteen-minute breaks—one in the morning and the other in the afternoon, and lunch was a half hour. Our community dog, Whitey, used to love to come to school with us and recline close to the stove during the winter months. When school let out for the summer in June, there was always a family student picnic, which included running races and other games, and the food was always delicious.

By 1951, a new teacher arrived at our school, replacing Mabel Henry. Her name was Grace Foltz, who previously taught at the Furnace Run School. She was quite different in her teaching style, which enabled me to learn much better starting in the fifth grade. She was not as mean as Mrs. Henry, but still could be strict. She loved having family picnics for her students at any time. She remained as our teacher until the school's closing in 1954.

Bridgeburg School.

We obtained our religious training at the schoolhouse every Sunday with Flora Zellefrow as our teacher, who also played the piano as we sang hymns that even today I can still remember the words. Joseph Steffey, then his son Henry Steffey, and later grandson Jack Steffey continued with leadership for keeping this Sunday school alive. I believe John Moore was the president of the Sunday school union. Avanelle Lasher-Painter and Violet Lee were also Sunday school teachers.

We also had vacation Bible school during the summer. One year, Reverend ER Cunnings, a former missionary, was in charge of the Bible school. He also gave a service. Part of the service was when he pleaded for all of us kids to be saved and come forward to the altar, and he would save our very souls. He gazed at me and said, "Now, Bobby, come forth to the altar, and be saved." I said, "No way!" and stormed out of the school building, crying while running down the road toward our home. Rev. Cunnings gave chase after me, pleading to come back and be saved. I zoomed right past my mother in the front yard of our home and down over the riverbank with Rev. Cunnings still giving chase. I hid under a big willow tree along the river, still sobbing. Rev. Cunnings ran right past me and finally gave up and returned to my mother, and she asked what was going on. "Mrs. Whited, I just wanted to save Bobby's soul! So sorry that it offended him." He retreated to the school building, and eventually, I came away from my hiding place. My mother was not mad at me. I will never forget this.

Larry Whited with community dog, Whitey.

At the age of six, I also began to take violin lessons from local resident Ruth Cowan, who, at the time, was a college student at Indiana State Teachers College and lived with her mother and father, Robert and Alberta Cowan. Their residence was a short walk close to the school building. I took lessons for six years and ended up taking lessons from Roger Stone in Kittanning. I was doing well as a violinist at the time.

I was called a sissy by my brother, Larry, and other friends for taking violin lessons as I eyed everyone else outside playing baseball. So I quit the violin lessons—a decision that, to this day, I still regret.

Bridgeburg School many years later.

Fishing in the river was so prominent, especially in the early spring when suckers (a breed of fish) were most sought after. Some of the adults fished as well. Fires blazed, and many stories were told and retold. It is a good remembrance I still carry with me today.

School Days—Myers School

Before there was a Bridgeburg School, there was a school where all Bridgeburg kids went called Myers School, named after the Myers family. It was located about a half mile west on the Quigley Hill Road. I remember Ms. Bessie Hooks, who was the teacher in this one-room brick schoolhouse for many years until it was closed in (I believe) 1952 or 1953. Then those kids were transferred to the Bridgeburg School until the Bridgeburg School was closed in 1954.

A2 • TUESDAY, JANUARY 16, 2018 — *Kittanning Leader Times*

GLIMPSE OF THE PAST
MYERS' SCHOOL, CIRCA 1910

Ray Tarr of North Buffalo, submitted this photograph of his grandfather, Raymond Tarr, who was one of the students that attended Myers' School, near Bridgeburg. The photograph was taken circa 1910. This photograph was first printed in the Leader Times in 1970. Members of the class were (front, from left) Thomas Schaub, Thomas Myers, Clarence Schaub, Raymond Tarr, Leas Whited, Lizzie Brison, Florence Richey, Chambers Claypoole, Earl Richey, Ida Lasher and Daniel Zellefrow; (second row) Hazel Schaub, Marie Wolfe, Annie Hooks, Margaret Steffey, Eliza Hoots, Helen Wolfe, Annabelle Hooks, Bernice Richey, Dorothy Lasher, Lettie Montgomery, Annie Rebold, Rosie Claypoole, Alma Cousins, Ethel Claypoole, Florence Patton, Goldie Patton, Hazel Whited, Annie Toy and Margaret Myers; (third row) Frank Lasher, Lloyd Myers, Raymond Hooks, Meade Wolfe, Albert Heinrich, Joe Rebold, James Johns, Walter Steffey, Sharon Hooks, Hollis John, Frank Hockenberry, John Montgomery, Theodore Hooks, Glen Toy and Herbert Zellefrow; (back row) H. Quigley, teacher; Sadie Richey, Frances Elliot, Eva Hooks, Stella Roofner, Rosie Tarr, Martha Brison, Myrtle Myers, Mary Zellefrow and Nelda McDonald.

School Days—Bridgeburg School

Bridgeburg School, September 1922.

Parts of this photo are damaged. *Left to right, front row*: Homer Toy, Bee Cousins, Ted Steffey, Leslie Rebold, Hartzell Morrow, Edward Welch, Webb Whited, Henry Steffey, John Moyer, and John Slagle. *Row 2*: Lois Gardner, Isabell Cousins, Ruby Hooks, Dessie Cravenor, Elizabeth Rebold, Florence Cravenor, Randall Zellefrow, Juliebell Gray, Lois Morrow, William Freeman, Mabel Gardner, Robert Slagle, and Henry Toy. *Row 3*: Clarence Freeman, Winifred Morrow, Clark Freeman, Kenneth Welch, Helen Tatsak, Ruth Leasure, Ola Toy, Cecil Gray, Grace Moyer, Margaret Gray, Annie Tatsak, Josephine Hooks, and Stella Cravenor. *Back row*: Blanche Toy, Ethel Wolfe, Pluma Cousins, Margaret Croyle, Alma Cousins, Gladys Welch, Mary Hooks, Mildred Wolfe, and George Thompson, teacher.

Bridgeburg School 1936-37

Most of this photo is unidentified except for:
Row 2: 3rd from left is John Y. Hooks II
Row 3: 2nd from left is Grace Zellefrow
Row 4: 4th from left is Bill Tatsak and 5th from left is Tom Tatsak.

Bridgeburg School, 1945
First Grade
(L-R) Larry Whited, Merle Hooks, Nancy Johns and Junior Hooks.
Back is Mabel Henry, teacher

Bridgeburg School 1946 (students not identified) Mable Henry, teacher (back row)

Bridgeburg School, 1947.

Front row, left to right: Linda Reitz, Martha Johns, Dan Boring, Bob Whited, Glee Lash, Lloyd Myers, Mitzie Boring, Frank Hockenberry Jr., Keith Crowe, and Norma Johns. *Row 2*: Nancy Tatsak, Junior Hooks, Nancy Johns, Gene Shaffer, Larry Whited, Jean Hooks, Dorothy Wolfe, Charles Zimmerman, Alice Hooks, and June Schaub. *Row 3*: Dick Crowe, Bob Freeman, Ellen Lash, Bob Shaffer, Ronald Freeman, and Peggy Hepfl. *Back row*: Richard Johns, Donald Shaffer, Avanell Schaub, Edith Goldinger, Valeria Zimmerman, and Teacher Mabel Henry.

The school year of 1952 or 1953 was somewhat different in that the Myers School shut down, and all their students were transferred to our school, the Bridgeburg School. Some of those new students were Judy Johnston, Jim Buffington, Sarah "Sally" McDowall, the Cousins family, and more. We all became friends. I believe the Harold Walker family moved into the area at this time.

This lasted until 1954 when our Bridgeburg School closed permanently, and we were bused to the Whitesell School located on old Route 422 toward Worthington. Furnace Run and Pine Hill, Center Hill, and Walk Chalk also joined us at Whitesell to form this school that was for seventh and eighth graders. I was in the seventh grade at the time. Teachers were Mertie Wallwork and Anne Smith.

Something very significant happened at this time as Mitzie Boring and Judy Johnston, who were eighth graders, sent their song list into the popular TV game show *Name That Tune* in order to raise money to buy the school building and be used for a church and, perhaps, a community building. A contestant was chosen to play the song list the girls had submitted, and they did win the money needed to buy the building.

Girl Who Helped Buy Church Dies

Mitzie Ann Boring, 15-year-old daughter of Mr. and Mrs. Clarence W. Boring, Adrian RD 1, died yesterday in the West Penn Hospital following an illness of two months.

The Kittanning High School student was one of two Adrian area girls who submitted early in 1954 a list of hit tunes to a nationwide TV show and had their list judged as a winning combination of tunes which were used on the show later.

After receiving the cash award for submitting the winning list, Mitzie and her girl friend gave the money toward the purchase of the old Bridgeville School. The building at the time was being bought by the American Sunday School Union for use as a chapel.

Mitzie Boring's obituary.

Members of the Bridgeburg community wanted the building to be used as a community building also, where different groups like the Women's Club, the Hunting Club, and the United Brick and Clay Workers Local 788 and others could hold their meetings, which they did in the past. There was an objection, however, where some wanted it to remain a church only. There were many community meetings about this subject that went on and on, and finally, the community gave up, and it became a church only. The church was never successful.

The next year, Tarrtown shut down, and those students from the seventh and eighth grade joined us at Whitesell. I believe the Pinehill students went back to the Pinehill School. Those in the lower grades went to a new school called East Franklin Township. I was in the eighth grade this year, and Harry Fink was our teacher, along with Anne Smith.

We had our own football team, for which I played, called East Franklin Township that played the Kittanning area schools that were seventh and eighth graders. Mr. Fink was our coach. We also took a school trip to Washington DC and Gettysburg during our eighth grade.

Whitesell Pupils End Journey To Nation's Capitol

A trip to Washington, D.C., and Gettysburg was completed this morning by the eigthth grade graduates of Whitesell School.

From the time the group left here Wednesday morning until their return this morning, they traveled by chartered bus to Washington, where they visited the Bureau of Printing, Washington monument, White House, Federal Bureau of Investigation, the Capitol, Smithsonian Institute, Arlington cemetery and Gettysburg battlefield.

Harry Fink, the class teacher, William Best and Mrs. William Walls accompanied the class group, which included:

Danny Boring, Ronald Salsgiver, Donald Johnston, Eddie Anthony, Ronald Grafton, Lloyd Meyers, James Armstrong, Robert Whited, Bobby Moore, Ralph Gaggini, Marlin Guthrie, Kenny Lemmon, Howard Hetrick, Robert Brice, Danny Goldinger, Joseph Palinski.

Ruth Leard, Nancy Hogenmiller, Susan Toy, Donna Black, Melissa Fair, Joanne Wolfe, Anita Sparks, Donna Jean Bowser, Ann Shaffer, Judy Harmer, Pamela Scaife, Carol Smith.

Judy Greenawalt, Marlene Barnhart, Barbara Campbell, Nancy Mechling, Rose Walker, Glee Lash, Darla Denardo and Sally McDowell.

Whitesell School eighth-grade class trip to Washington DC and Gettysburg.

CHAPTER 7

Dredging of the River

Probably in the late 1940s dredging in the Allegheny River became quite common as the JK Davison Sand and Gravel giant dredge boat became present on the river, practically in our backyard. The noise it made was unbelievable as barges were filled with sand and gravel from the river bottom and transported to market by paddle wheelers, the Crescent and BD Rake. Sometimes the Crescent would tie up at our oak tree in our backyard. One day the cook from the Crescent came out and asked my brother Larry and me and Ron and Bob Freeman if we wanted some cookies. We said yes immediately, and he gave us large boxes of cookies—I mean large boxes!

The dredge boat also supplied employment for local residents. I believe Tom Tatsak retired there and probably more. I know Jack Steffey and Junior Steffey were also employed there, and Jack also survived a terrible accident while there as well. Arnold Weaver also was employed there, and I believe Art Luke also. As I recall, the dredging combed the whole pool between locks #7 and #8 and then went southward on the Allegheny. The dredging continued for many years.

The *Dredging Vessel Directory* claimed that in dredged areas of the river where the gravel supply was extracted, it caused populations of fish to be reduced. Researchers investigated pools in locks #7 and #8 near Kittanning and Templeton and came up with these results. I believe dredging in the Allegheny came to an end by 2013.

We were so accustomed to listening to the radio in the late '40s, especially to programs like the *Lone Ranger* and other heroes. The magic of television finally appeared, and the Hockenberry family was the first in Bridgeburg to obtain a TV set, probably in late 1949. Since no other family had television, they assigned several families a night when they could come into their home and watch this modern miracle. This was a nice gesture from the Hockenberrys. They also provided wiener roasts, or hot-dog roasts, for us kids, along with much singing.

My family didn't get our first TV set until 1952, right before the baseball World Series was to begin. We started out with a Bendix TV that just didn't work right, followed by a Crosley that made terrible noises, and finally, a Montgomery Ward set that worked fine with a good picture. You see, back then in Bridgeburg, there was only one TV station; it was the old WDTV from Pittsburg, which was part of the Dumont Television Network. Later on, two additional TV stations arrived for all television networks.

All reception came from our antenna, which was tied to the chimney on our roof. Sometimes, the wind itself would play a big part in our reception as it seemed to blow our signal away.

I can still remember my father on top of the roof during a snowstorm, turning the antenna, trying to get better reception so he could watch the *Friday Night Fights*. He would communicate with my mother who was in the house, at the opened living-room window, telling him if the picture was better or not. Johnstown, Pennsylvania, also had a TV channel that we all tried to get that needed an all-different antenna. My dad used a curtain rod and lead in wire for this antenna, which seemed to work somewhat after he failed at a makeshift antenna using my music stand. Remember, this was many years away from cable TV and all the rest of the niceties we enjoy today.

CHAPTER 8

Haws Refractories

John H. Rebold was the original builder of the brickyard later to become Haws Refractories. I can say that Haws Refractories was the major employer of all Bridgeburg residents. It was called a brickyard, but eventually developed into more diverse products that were urgently needed by steel mills, especially for the war effort during World War II.

Haws Refractories.

My father was a pugger and was responsible for mixing different types of clays that went into a brick machine and onto a cutting table where a correct size of a column was cut at a cutting machine. Then the slug was conveyed onto the presses where the ware was formed by the pressmen and was then stored for a drying process in tunnels. From there the ware was transferred to the setting gang who set the ware into kilns that were later fired to bake the ware. From there the wheeling gang used Hi-Lifts, originally wheelbarrows, to load the ware into railroad cars, and off to market it went, up the Shawmut spur and onto the B&O Railroad. These, of course, were just the basics of links to the production.

A headline dated February 4, 1944, indicated that sixty-five workers at Haws Refractories terminated a two-day walkout after the War Labor Board approved raises for the workers.

Probably around 1950, a new superintendent arrived at the yard. His name was Bill Woods, and he replaced Mack McGeary. Woods was from the St. Louis, Missouri, area and what we could call somewhat flamboyant. He, his wife, and son, Robert, lived temporarily in the office building. Woods immediately bought a new, bright-red Oldsmobile convertible and played the role of the superintendent. He was well-liked, though. The production foremen at the time for two shifts were my uncle

Early brickyard employees in front of the kiln, *(left to right)* Deemer Heginbotham, Clyde Heginbotham, Melvin Heginbotham (father of Deemer and Clyde), Raymond Tarr, and Mr. Gibson, the boss.

Carl Whited and Walter "Wick" Steffey. I, too, after my stint in the Navy, worked at the yard for two years, from 1964–1966. The yard met its demise in, I believe, 1973. It did provide employment for many with decent wages for many years. I can also remember that my cousin Lester "Leck" Hooks was also a superintendent following Bill Woods, and Bill Pleacher was superintendent when I worked there.

I grew up not knowing exactly what my father did at the yard. But after I became employed there, I soon found out. The pugger was responsible, as I said earlier, for mixing the different types of clays and starting all the presses and lighting at the beginning of the shift. One morning I was doing labor work with what was called shaving nozzles. The foreman, Bud Mohney, came into the shop and gave the order for my dad to "start 'em up!" My dad remained motionless except for a spat of chewing tobacco. Mohney returned and proclaimed, "Webb, I said to start 'em up." My dad replied, "I'm not starting anything up until you get the correct lighting in order for these men to do their job." In no time, maintenance men came with ladders and installed new lights to brighten the shop so the workers could see better. Mohney then returned and said, "Webb, are you now ready to start 'em up?" "I am now," Dad replied with another spat of tobacco. He looked down at me and gave me a wink as if to say, "This is how things are done here, son." Dad was the financial secretary for United Brick and Clay Workers Local 788 for many years.

There also was a clay mine attached to the brickyard, supplying them with the much-needed clay used in their products. The mine superintendent was John Painter. Early on, mules were used to transport the clay from the mines. As a youngster, I can recall the mules escaping and miners chasing them. There was a mule barn located close to the mines. Little of it remains. Later, electric motorcars were used to replace the mules.

There was a clay tipple where bad clay was dumped using rails and clay cars to escalate the clay up the tipple and dumped. Charlie Lockhart manned that job.

Finally, the mines seemed to peter out, and so then the clay was trucked in from Northern Pennsylvania locales. I can recall one time when John Painter asked my dad to tour the mines on the motorcar. My brother, Larry, and I went along, and it truly was a thrilling experience as we seemed to travel miles underground into the mines.

CHAPTER 9

Snowstorm, Sled Riding, Poker Games, and Trains

It was Thanksgiving Day, November 23, 1950, and I was nine years old. Thanksgiving was a great day for me and my family, which included my mother and father and my brother, and we had a guest that day, Clair Cloak. It was a pleasant day with a fine feast and many reasons for giving thanks. I believe my father and brother, Larry, went rabbit hunting with Jay Hockenberry earlier in the day. We had no television at the time, but I listened to *Dragnet* on the radio that evening. During the late evening or early morning snow started to fall.

It was Friday morning, and we didn't have school because of the Thanksgiving holiday. My father worked night shift at the local brickyard, and on Fridays we all went to Kittanning for our groceries. My brother, Larry, and I were hoping to take in a matinee at the movies. Before we piled into our maroon 1946 Plymouth, I had an early snowball fight with Frankie Hockenberry. I just loved to see the snow come down, and by then, snow had started to accumulate. We rushed to Kittanning, which was a five-mile trip. Bob Cowan, our neighbor, requested to go along for his groceries. My parents and Mr. Cowan purchased their weekly supply of groceries and hurried back home because of all the snow that had continued to fall and no tire chains on our car. There was no time for a movie matinee.

The snow kept pelting down with no end in sight. We arrived home safely. My dad walked to work that evening as always, being the brickyard was close to our residence. What weather news we received was from the radio in between the *Lone Ranger* and other favorite radio programs. The weather reports were not great, and the snow kept tumbling down. On awakening Saturday, November 25, 1950, we could not believe our eyes! It was still snowing. My dad returned home from work and measured twenty-three inches of snow in our yard. He was called out later to shovel the roofs over the brick ware because of the fear of weight and collapse of those roofs or sheds from the heavy snowfall. By Sunday, the snow stopped completely, but school was cancelled on Monday and the rest of the week. This was truly the best part of the snowstorm. Everything was shut down. In those days snow removal was not as advanced as today, and they didn't use salt.

Since then, it has been called the Great Appalachian Snowstorm of 1950 or the Great Thanksgiving Snowstorm. Nearly thirty inches of snow covered Pittsburgh, and two feet or more blanketed Cleveland. It affected twenty-two states. Power was out to more than one million customers, three hundred fifty-three people died as a result of the storm, and it caused $66.7 million in damages (in 1950 dollars). People could not leave their homes for days. Milk and bread delivery trucks could not get through. School buses were halted, and it was a joyous occasion for all students—no school!

The Great Thanksgiving Snowstorm of 1950, *(front)* Bob Whited, (back) Larry Whited.

One wintery Friday evening, probably in 1951, my brother, Larry, and I were on our way to walk about a half mile in the snow along the River Road to get our haircut from Art Luke. Delp Tarr came along with a sleighlike wagon with wooden rails that hauled coal and was driven by his horses, Bill and Roy. He asked if we wanted to go along to take the last of his coal to the Abe Myers coal mines. We jumped in. It was a night to remember as the country winter scenery with the snow as a background was beautiful. We made a right turn on the old Patton Road by the Katie Gray home and proceeded onward across the railroad tracks, past the reservoir, and onto the old Orie Patton house and beyond to the old coal mines. It was snowing more at the time.

Our 1946 Plymouth in the 1950 snowstorm.

Delp left off the remainder of the coal at the Myers mines and proceeded on to the Quigley Hill Road where Larry and I jumped off. We barely made it on time for our haircuts. It was a night of remembrance that we never forgot, riding with Delp and the horses through a most scenic snow-covered landscape.

Sled Riding

In the winter months when there was a lot of snow and everyone had a sled, off we would go to the hills at the Bridgeburg schoolhouse. We would go to the top of the hill facing the schoolhouse where there was a grassy field. With speeds too fast to comprehend, we sped down this slope, hoping to make a fast right turn into the schoolhouse or, sometimes unable to stop or make the turn, plunge into the school-bus turn-around. I believe Ronnie Freeman made that plunge with snow falling and unable to see clearly.

In the fall when the leaves were falling, we didn't need any snow for sledding. We used old seats from the school desks as sleds as we came down that same hill with the fallen leaves to propel us just as fast as if we were on snow.

We used to play on the large rocks on the west side of the schoolhouse where there were lots of wild grapevines growing. One evening, Gene Shaffer thought he was Tarzan and stood on the tallest rock that happened to have a grapevine nearby. He did his Tarzan yell, grabbed the grapevine, and swung, not knowing if the vine would hold him or not. Luckily, the vine did hold him, and he survived. For a while, I thought he was a goner!

Poker Games

In the summertime, men in the community enjoyed their poker games on Sunday. There could be a knock on our door on Sunday mornings, and there would be Jim Johns asking for my dad. His message would be, "Webb, let's get a little game going." Those men included Jim Johns, my dad, Mutt Freeman, Bricky Heinrich, and Ted Hooks Sr. and maybe more. Also included in the games might have been Bitty Tarr, Bub Tarr, and Lee Zellefrow. They would retreat to an area along the hillside railroad spur where they used railroad ties in a square formation for their seats and nail kegs for their tables. For their thirsts, beer was taken with them. Those Sunday morning gatherings went on for years.

The Ins and Outs of the Outhouse
(An excerpt from an article written by Bob Whited for the Warren *Tribune Chronicle*, September, 2005)

We had the humblest of all sanitation systems. Yes, that means an outhouse! There was much rejoicing for our small family when our spanking new indoor bathroom was constructed in the middle 1950s. I was fifteen at the time and can still remember quite well the difference it made—the thirty-yard dash in the middle of the night became no more. For those who never experienced this type of reality and way of life, you can be awfully glad you never did. Spiders spinning their webs within the outhouse, along with wasp nests, and flies by the squadrons seemed always there to greet you during the summer months. Getting stung was part of the visit, and of all places to get stung!

Along with that came that distinctive odor. In the winter months, it was the cold and the rain and freezing rain and the ice and the snow and the door that (due to the weather) was frozen shut with ice and required attention to gain entrance. The seat itself got mighty cold on those wintry nights. At nighttime, the dark bleak setting usually required a flashlight. You became quite angry and agitated when you discovered that your flashlight batteries were dead as you hastily stumbled out for your visit.

The outhouse, though, seems to always have an enduring affection as part of rural life in those early days. It was all that you had, and we all seemed to make the most of it and were glad to have it. The Sears Roebuck and Co. or Montgomery Ward's catalogs usually graced the outhouse for "toilet paper," and as page 450 came around, it was time for a new catalog! Some people, however, (my family included) were well stocked with real toilet paper.

Ours had a tin roof, and when it rained, the roof produced a sound out of this world! It was like being entertained during your visit.

A Copperhead Story

I was probably seven years old when floating rumors were told that a sour cherry tree existed along the River Road, near the river, and was loaded with the prized fruit that made those delicious cherry pies. As I recall, the tree was located just north of the Rebold farm road. Bob and Ronnie Freeman, Larry, and I decided that this was our project to go and pick those cherries so our mothers could bake scrumptious pies. So off we went with our pails, and sure enough upon arrival, the tree was all the rumors proclaimed as it was loaded with the ripened fruit.

We all decided to climb the tree and pick those beauties. We picked some, and suddenly, I believe Bob startled us all by screaming that a giant copperhead was coiled just under the tree. We all decided to jump over the snake and run to the railroad tracks. One by one, everyone jumped except me. I was afraid to jump because I didn't know whether I would jump far enough to clear the snake. Eventually, I managed to jump and cleared the copperhead!

Being I was the youngest and smallest of the group, the others checked for a snake bite, and sure enough, I had a mark on my leg that resembled fang marks. "What should we do?" Bob decided the best bet was to use his penknife and cut the area in my leg and suck the blood, along with the assumed poison, out of my leg and save my life, which they did.

They practically carried me the whole way back home with me crying, and as my mother was standing in the front yard, the story was told. On examination, my mother determined that it was just a berry bush scratch and not fang marks. Very few cherries were picked that day, but my life was saved. Just another Bridgeburg adventure!

Sounds of the Trains

While lying in bed at night, we were lulled to sleep by the locomotives of three trains passing through. They all had a distinctive whistle. The trains were the Midnight Flyer on the B&O, the Coal Drag on the Shawmut, and the Pennsy on the tracks on the other side of the Allegheny River.

Shawmut locomotive
(photo by Randy Kiser).

CHAPTER 10

Bridgeburg Women's Club, Schools, Baseball, Swimming, and More

The Bridgeburg Women's Club was formed in, I believe, 1951 by Velma "Dot" Luke and Edna Mateer. This was a service club and social club, and membership grew immediately. As kids, we still remember their famous apple-butter project that was made at the home of member Belva Painter. They usually met at the schoolhouse, later in their homes. A huge pot of apples and great seasonings were stirred constantly by the ladies. The pot was fired up by a kindling-wood fire. You could smell the apple butter from a long distance away. They also made quilts and many other service projects. My mother, Madge Whited, was a charter member. This club lasted until the 1980s and did outstanding work not only for the Bridgeburg community, but for other communities as well.

Bridgeburg Women's Club. Pictured (L-R) Velma "Dot" Luke, unidentified, Marlene Chasse, Debbie Crissman and Madge Whited

Bridgeburg Women's Club—Christmas 1980
Front: Pluma Duncan, Alma Zellefrow, and Edna Mateer. *Back:* Sarabell Long, Muriel Beckett, Madge Whited, Velma "Dot" Luke, Marlene Chasse, Phyllis Wolfe, and Martha Walker

Bridgeburg Women's Club News
(Courtesy of the *Kittanning Leader Times*)

Summertime swimming in the river was an important part of all our lives. I believe around 1952, my dad and Frank Cloak erected a diving board in the river. The board came from under our back porch, and this diving board attracted many adults and kids. This diving board remained for many years. Eventually, we had to take the board away because of the heavy flooding and ice throughout the fall and winter months.

Baseball was the sport that we all idolized at that time. We formed a team when I was thirteen years old at Tarrtown, and I also played for East Franklin Township in a PONY league. We played our games at West Kittanning and Kittanning.

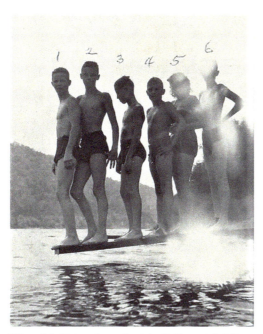

The old diving board with *(left to right)* Ron Freeman, Bob Freeman, Bob Whited, Dan Boring, Mitzie Boring, and Larry Whited.

Baseball clipping featuring Bob Whited and Dan Boring (courtesy of Kittanning *Leader Times*).

Danny Boring and I joined this team along with Danny's cousin Denny Garland. I pitched most of those games. The next year we formed an Armstrong County Junior League sandlot team at Adrian, where different area players became our team. Nelson "Fat" Milligan and Bud Boring were our managers. This was the first time we really played organized baseball. This went on for two years. There was an earlier Bridgeburg baseball field alongside the Shawmut railroad tracks near the Aidah Hepfl home. There was a Bridgeburg team of boys older than me who played there. We later graduated into the Armstrong County Senior League, where I played for Toy's Crossroads in 1959 and with Bob Freeman in 1960 on the Kittanning Refractories team before enlisting in the Navy. After my hitch in the Navy, I played for Tarrtown.

My cousin Lester "Leck" Hooks made it to the minor leagues and is a member of the Armstrong County Sports Hall of Fame. Leck married Doris Hawk-Hooks (08-20-1926 to 05-11-2009). Their children were David Wolfe (stepson), Linda Hooks-Cornman, and Kimberly Hooks-Pivetta. Chamie Hooks was also a good baseball player from Bridgeburg.

Small-game hunting season in Bridgeburg was like a holiday. When I became of age, my father bought me a new shotgun. At that time, game was very plentiful, and fresh-cooked rabbit and squirrel were delicious as my mother new how to cook wild game. Deer season came later after Thanksgiving. In today's world, the whole Bridgeburg hunting area and all the areas around it are posted, and it is unlawful to hunt there. What a shame.

I never will forget the spring and summer of 1953 as my brother, Larry, and Bob Freeman both purchased beagle puppies for hunting season. Our dog was called Lady, and Bob's dog was called Apache or Pach. Those two pups played together all summer long and gave us many laughs as they got into funny situations and mischief down on the river shore. They both became good hunters. Ronnie Freeman also got a cocker spaniel puppy called Lucky that got killed on the river road.

Lady and Pach playing in our backyard.

Left to right: Dan Boring with Pach, Denny Garland, Bob Whited with Lady, and Ron Freeman with mongrel pup from the Hockenberrys.

Trout season also became a big thing, starting when I was twelve years old. Laverne Wolfe, who was my cousin Doris's husband, schooled me well on how to fish for trout. We fished together for many years along with Bob Freeman, Dan Boring, and other neighbor kids. We had a lot of fun with long walks to Pine Creek and many fish stories that we might never forget. Laverne was all of us kids' big brother along with Jack Cloak. Laverne not only hunted and fished with us, but he also taught us the fine art of marble shooting.

Catch of the day! Mitzie Boring, Larry Whited, Dan Boring with the catch of the day, Frank Hockenberry, and Bob Whited.

We also became trappers as muskrats were in abundance and a much-wanted fur. We all learned to trap at an early age and learned to skin and stretch our pelts. We then sent them to Sears and Roebuck who paid a good price for our hard work. We even had competition from adult trappers. Trapping is something you never hear about in this modern age. We had to check our traps often even in the evening darkness and the early morning.

My grandfather passed away in March 1953 at the age of eighty-nine, almost ninety. He never had running water or a bathroom in his entire life. He was born in 1863 during the Civil War. As a youngster, I would often visit him and my aunts Hazel and Nora. He loved to tell ghost stories that scared me to death and sometimes made me afraid to walk home at night.

One time, Bob, Larry, and I found a honeybee tree close to Buck's Point and in the Rich Hollow area. We told my grandfather of our quest to bring him some fresh honey—how we battled the bees and got in the hollow tree and brought our treasure of honey (that was really spoiled) for my grandfather's inspection. He told us that we should not have bothered those bees and called our honey a foul brood.

A Visit from Aunt Molly

In the summer of 1952, my grandfather and my aunts Hazel and Nora got some delightful news that my grandfather's sister Mary "Molly" Whited-Leas would be visiting. They hadn't seen each other for years. Aunt Molly had distinguished herself many times as an owner of numerous hotels in Philadelphia, Florida, and Bakersfield, California. Most of the family in the Bridgeburg area could hardly wait to greet and meet the lady they heard so much about. I will never forget that day when her entourage arrived, which consisted of Aunt Molly; her daughter, Maude Thompson; my grandfather's half brother, Dave McElravy; and family members Irene Karns and Lizzie Mechling.

Left to right, front: Bob Freeman, Bob Whited, and Larry Whited. *Row 2:* Elnora Whited, John Wesley Whited, Molly Whited-Leas, Irene Karns, Lizzie Mechling, and Ruby Freeman. *Row 3:* Edna Whited-Hooks, Dave McElravy, Carl Whited, Maude Thompson, Hazel Whited, and Webb Whited.

It was a day of celebration. They had so much to talk about!

Left to right: John Wesley Whited, Maude Thompson, and Molly Whited-Leas.

My uncle Carl was also famous for his scary ghost stories. His eyes alone, while telling these fabled tales, gave an even scarier effect to the stories. I believe my aunt Cass used to warn him about scaring us to death. He loved telling those stories.

One time, my uncle Carl went on vacation to visit his daughter Betty in Michigan. I was trusted to take care of his dog, Nellie, who was a basset hound. One morning I went to feed old Nellie, and she had died during the evening. I felt so bad. I had to bury the dog. My brother and Danny Boring sang hymns while I buried the dog. My uncle Carl was very understanding when he returned home and found out about Nellie.

Berry picking was also one of our many events in the summertime. We picked raspberries, blackberries, and huckleberries (native blueberries). My mother made delicious pies and jellies and jams. All the berries were always plentiful.

I remember one time when my brother, Larry, and I and Bud Anderson decided to make money, picking and selling huckleberries to the community. We did well as we picked water buckets full of berries. One mistake we made was that we picked and sold berries to Jay Mateer. Little did we know that those berries we picked were from Mr. Mateer's own property. My dad made us return the money we made back to the Mateers. Mr. Mateer refused the money, though, and didn't really care.

My brother, Larry, peddled the weekly paper called the *Grit*. During this time, one of his customers, Bob Cowan, passed away, and the calling hours were at the Cowan home. No one knew that Mr. Cowan had an identical twin brother who was visiting for his brother's funeral. When Larry delivered the paper to the Cowan home, the twin brother opened the door, and Larry thought he had seen a ghost and ran the whole way home.

Gardening became a hobby for all of us at a very young age. We all claimed our spots along the riverbank and actually grew some good vegetables. The muskrats and groundhogs also loved our vegetables, sorry to say.

The farmers of Bridgeburg, like the Tarrs and the Myers, the Schaubs and the Hooks and the Rebolds, the Pattons, and Haines Zellefrow, farmed their lands by sowing their seeds, raising chickens and livestock, shearing their sheep and butchering their hogs, and raising vegetables and fruit and much more. This was a different era. They did it the hard way without modern-day machinery.

Floods were always a big fear along the Allegheny, especially in the early spring or late winter when the ice went out. Our home was close to the river, and the water and the ice came close several times. I recall the spring of 1959 when the ice cakes came up into our backyard. Older residents claim that the 1936 flood was the biggest of the floods.

How high's the water Mama? On the Allegheny River.
Left to right: Madge Whited and Mary Boring.

Building so-called cabins was also part of summertime fun. One time, in particular, we built an underground cabin just north of our homes along the Shawmut Railroad tracks. Those involved in this building included Bob and Ron Freeman; my brother, Larry; Ron Lasher; Dan Boring; and me. First, a hole was dug, and then railroad ties were placed on top with grass sods placed on top of the ties for a roof. Entrance and exit holes were then dug, and even a brick floor was installed. This was a terrible mistake, for there was little air in this space, and we were unable to breathe.

Halloween was a bit different in that we somewhat became pranksters throwing hardened field corn at people's windows. The older boys went a lot further and did some mischievous acts like overturning outhouses. We did, however, dress up and travel from house to house for our candy treats, which were many.

Everyone seemed to go to Jim and Clarence Johns's home in the evenings. They seemed to love our company. We (JY Hooks II, Tasker Hooks, Gump Hooks, Chamie Hooks, and many of us younger kids) spent many jovial evenings at the Johns's home. Jim passed away in 1957 and had a wooden leg. How he lost his leg, I would assume probably in an accident. I should know, but I don't. He worked at the brickyard until his death in 1957.

Larry and Ronnie Freeman were aware that Junior Hooks was a bit afraid in the dark. One night he was at the Johns's home, and Larry and Ronnie decided how they would scare Junior that evening. They made a dummy and put clothes on it and went on the bridge, and when Junior was on his way home, as he walked under the bridge, they dropped the dummy right in front of him. The dummy also had a rope around its neck. Junior was so scared that he ran to Lee Zellefrow's house and straight through the screen door without opening it. That was being scared!

Jack Cloak was a lot older than the rest of us. He played football and baseball with us and even hide-and-seek and other games. He was really our "big brother."

I believe, in the early 1950s, a gas well was drilled on the Frank Hiwiller lot now owned by Haws Refractories or the brickyard. After the framework was complete, the drillers came, and drilling began. It attracted us kids who were interested in how all this worked. The drillers were very friendly and allowed us to watch them work. It seemed to take months before gas was found or struck. The drillers used to bring up a lot of water and sludge and dumped it in what was called a sump hole. One afternoon, after the drillers were gone, Danny Boring and I were at the well site. While walking on the outside of the well frame, Danny fell and plunged right into the sump hole. I watched in fear, wondering whether he would get out. Finally, I saw just a bump in the sludge as he appeared with all that sludge on him. He had to swim out and ran home as fast as possible. This was a very scary event. He was all right, though.

My brother, Larry, could be a very mischievous kid at school. One day our teacher Mabel Henry was instructing one of the grades on an upcoming project. Larry sneaked into the cloakroom and put on Mrs. Henry's coat and hat with a veil and then stood behind her to imitate her while she taught. The whole school began laughing, and she couldn't understand why until she turned around and saw Larry with her own duds on, mocking her. I believe Larry got a heavy spanking. That's when spanking was allowed in school.

In 1959, a decision was made to do major repairs on the River Road to pave it and straighten it out. At the time, from the Jay Mateer home north to Reesedale, it still was a dirt road. A construction company by the name Rathbid and Gore got the contract. Another company came in first and cleared all the trees and brush. The big turn at Clarence Johns's home was eliminated and completely straightened out and paved. By the end of summer most of the work was completed. What a difference.

CHAPTER 11

Pages from the Past

(Courtesy of the *Kittanning Leader Times*)

Bridgeburg News

Mr. and Mrs. Robert McElwain, of Spring Church, are rejoicing over the arrival of a young daughter. Mrs. McElwain was formerly Miss Annabel Hooks, of this place.

Mr. and Mrs. Jay Mateer and children, spent Saturday evening with the latter's parents, Mr. and Mrs. Thomas McAuley, of Route 1, Adrian.

Joe Steffey is suffering from an attack of asthma.

June Montgomery is visiting her grandparents, Mr. and Mrs. Ed Lasher, of near French's Corners.

Miss Julia Gray who had been quite ill is able to be about again.

Mrs. Laura Claypool, of Adrian, was here Monday evening.

Miss Bessie Hooks who spent her vacation in this place has returned to Loes Creek, Kentucky.

Mr. and Mrs. John Cousins, Jr., and son Jack, spent Saturday evening in Kittanning.

Miss Helen Hooks, of Applewold, is spending a couple weeks with her grandparents, Mr. and Mrs. J. Y. Hooks.

Henry Steffer had his tonsils removed Monday evening.

Mrs. John Cousins, Sr., and daughter, Isabel, visited on Sunday with the former's daughter, Mrs. Amos Howard, of Templeton.

Mr. and Mrs. Turl Delp and son, Ronald, accompanied by Mrs. Weldin Delp and son, Turl, of Monaca, spent Sunday with Marlin Cochran.

John Gray is recovering from an attack of mumps.

Mr. and Mrs. John Whited and children, of East Brady, were the week-end guests of Wesley Whited and Mrs. Alex Hooks.

Mrs. Etla Coak and Miss Ethel and "Billy" Wynkoop, of Cowansville, visited relatives here Monday evening.

The Misses Mary and Eva Hooks are spending their vacations with friends in Covington, Ky.

S. F. Williams is on the sick list.

Miss Ola Toy has returned from Mrs. Henry Stouffer, of French's Corners.

Mrs. Mary Koladish attended the funeral of John Shesheba at Brookville Sunday.

Mr. and Mrs. Joe Steffey and daughter, Mrs. Margaret Emelton were shoppers in Butler Saturday evening.

Mrs. Ona Patton was in Kittanning Saturday.

Tell advertisers you saw their ads in The Leader-Times

July 26, 1929

Bridgeburg News

Mr. and Mrs. Curtis Toy and children of near Adrian, spent Sunday at the home of Mr. and Mrs. Harry Hooks.

Mrs. Adeline Roofner of Tarrtown visited on Sunday at the Joseph Wolfe home.

Merle and Eddy Elgin, of Kittanning, were here last week the guests of Mr. and Mrs. Alex Hooks.

Marlin Cochran spent the week-end with relatives in Pittsburg.

Miss Alice Rebold who suffered a severe attack of illness last week is reported very much improved.

Miss Margaret Unger, of Widnoon and Mrs. Audley Gray of Adrian, Route 1 visited relatives in this place on Monday.

Mr. and Mrs. Samuel Croyle and children motored to French's Corners on Sunday and spent the day with Mr. and Mrs. I. D. Leasure.

Mr. and Mrs. Joe Steffey and son Gene and Mrs. Ralph Gray and Mrs. William Heinrich and Mr. George Rebold motored to Parker on Sunday and attended the funeral of William Sullivan who died in Pittsburg on Friday of last week.

Miss Elnora Whited spent Friday evening in Kittanning.

Many friends and acquaintances in this vicinity learned with regret on Wednesday of the death of Ben Lockhart of Mosgrove. Mr. Lockhart was drowned while at work at lock and dam No. 8 at Orr Hill.

November 2, 1929

CHAPTER 12

At Present

The years seemed to fly by, and in no time, we were in Kittanning High School and becoming more adult as graduation neared. Bob Freeman was drafted into the Army. Dan Boring played high-school football and then went off to college. Later he married Kathy Turner, and they have two children: Carol and Amy. Dan presently lives in the Cleveland, Ohio, area. Early on in his working career, Larry worked for NUMEC, which was a nuclear plant that eventually (in my opinion and that of others) gave him bad health. He married Loretta Doyle from West Leechburg, and they had three children: Carla Whited-Sims, Michael, and Brett. Larry died in 2016 and Michael died April, 2018. Ronnie stayed around Bridgeburg and married Sandra Greenawalt. They lived in West Kittanning and had three children: Debbie Freeman-Sanders, Randy Freeman, and Michael Freeman. Sandy was killed in an auto accident. Ronnie has also passed on.

Laverne and Doris Wolfe also had three children: Teri Wolfe-Hollern, Janet Wolfe-Campbell, and Kim Wolfe-Hufhand. Laverne has passed on, and Doris now lives in Kittanning. Lloydie Myers married Sandra Foster-Myers, had children, and eventually moved to Ellwood City. He owned a portable-toilet company. His wife recently passed away. Junior Hooks married Nancy Campbell and remained on the Hooks farm. He has also passed on. They had five children. Jack Cloak married Etta Croyle and had four children: William Cloak, Lisa Cloak-Slagle, Nancy Cloak-Greenawalt, and Amy Cloak-Crissman. Jack has passed on. Ron Lasher, last I heard, contracted Alzheimer's and, at present, is in a nursing home.

Homer and George Painter have passed on. Bob Freeman presently resides in West Kittanning. As far as I know, all the Hockenberry family have passed on. Frank Jr. and Eddie Joe both were killed in auto accidents.

I enlisted in the Navy in 1960 and returned home in 1964. I worked at the brickyard for two years and then moved to Ohio to work for General Motors in Lordstown. I married Joyce Toussaint from Ford City in 1967. We have four children: Lisa Whited-Snyder, Lori Whited-Neidlinger, Rob Whited, and Todd Whited. I am now retired and still living in Austintown, Ohio. I also write a column for the Warren (Ohio) *Tribune Chronicle*.

Bridgeburg today is sort of a ghost town to what it was when I was growing up there. The brickyard is long gone. The schoolhouse has fallen over. Very little of the past is still present. The row of houses that we lived in has been gone since the 1980s, replaced by a forest of trees. Most of the early homes are gone, especially the one I was born in. The West Mosgrove railroad station is also long gone. Almost all residents have passed on, but left their mark in this tiny hamlet. It is so sad while driving along the River Road to see Bridgeburg today compared to the community I knew and loved as a child.

That giant bridge, though, still remains! It has stood tall since 1899. It is much too dangerous to walk on, and the decking and walkways have been closed down.

Bridgeburg Schoolhouse (taken in November 2019).

The brickyard, as mentioned before, completely shut down and dismantled in the early 1970s. Edwin Slick, who was the owner at the time, left it run-down, and it went bankrupt. Everyone lost their pensions. What a calamity!

Edwin E. Slick Jr.

Edwin E. Slick Jr., 79, a Pittsburgh native and retired board chairman and president of the former Haws Refractory Co. in Johnstown, Cambria County, died yesterday of a heart attack at Mercy Hospital, Johnstown.

Mr. Slick, of Johnstown, was a member of the Duquesne Club, Pittsburgh Athletic Club, Ye Olde Country Club in Johnstown, North East River Yacht Club, North East, Md., and the Wellwood Yacht Club of Charlestown, Md.

He also was a member of the Notre Dame Club and the First Lutheran Church of Johnstown.

Surviving is his wife, Ella.

A private graveside service will be held Monday in Homewood Cemetery.

Edwin E. Slick Jr.'s obituary.

Oh, it is still called Bridgeburg and is still indicated by an entrance sign as well. Most of the people are new and young, whom I have never met or heard of, and they have never met or heard of me, naturally. The Junior Hooks family still remains there, though, as a tribute to the past and also the future.

Today, the Allegheny River still flows past the village of Bridgeburg and has collected many stories and memories along its way. It has been dredged and strengthened by dams or locks, but still is *la belle riviere*, or "the beautiful river."

The B&O Railroad, after many years of service, merged with CSX Transportation on August 31, 1987. As far as I can tell, the great bridge was still in use as late as 2018. Perhaps, it still is.

The Pittsburg and Shawmut main from Brockway to Brookville has been removed. These lines are officially what they call railbanked and can be put back in operation in the future if needed, including the Bridgeburg rails.

The power plant at Reesedale received coal by way of the railroad until it was announced in January 2012 that the plant would be closing. It is believed the last coal train to the plant ran in February 2012.

The old Myers-Patton Cemetery on top of Quigley Hill is still there and holds most of the early residents. Many are veterans, who fought for our country, and many relatives as well. Many had made this early farmland a place to live, raise their families, till the soil, and live their lives with pride while living the simple life. They did it well. In this present fast-paced world when everything must be done right now, we must show respect to this era in Bridgeburg when the simple life was so valuable, and most of us yearn for it to return.

Myers-Patton Cemetery

Miscellaneous Photos

Author, Bob Whited, with his wife, Joyce Toussaint-Whited (March 1995).

Bob and Joyce Whited's children—Todd E. Whited, Lori L. Whited-Neidlinger, Lisa A. Whited-Snyder, and Robert J. (Rob) Whited.

Lawrence E. (Larry) Whited with his wife,
Loretta Doyle-Whited (1988).

Larry and Loretta Doyle-Whited's children—Brett Whited,
Carla Sims-Whited, and Michael Whited.

Teri Wolfe-Hollern, daughter of
Laverne and Doris Whited-Wolfe.

Janet Wolfe-Campbell, daughter of
Laverne and Doris Whited-Wolfe.

Kim Wolfe-Hufhand, daughter of Laverne
and Doris Whited-Wolfe.

Hazel Whited and Jola Roofner.

Clair Cloak, a friend of my family and of all of Bridgeburg.

Bob and Ron Freeman and Larry Whited with dog Buck.

Gretta Cousins, Margaret Cousins, and Hazel Whited.

Future mechanics!
Bob Freeman and Larry Whited (sitting on the car) and Ron Freeman (standing).

Ready to help with WWII!
(Left–right) Larry Whited and
Bob and Ron Freeman.

Carrie Moore.

Jack Hooks and dog Sandy.

Bob Whited, always wanting to be a sailor and eventually did join the US Navy, 1960–1964.

Bob Whited and Aunt Hazel Whited sitting on Granddad's bench.

Company on the Whited's back porch (late 1940s).

Shawmut Line caboose.

The End!

ACKNOWLEDGMENTS

It is certainly my pleasure to acknowledge those who have helped in this project. Without you, this history of Bridgeburg would have been nearly impossible to write.

Thank you!

John Atherton
Lori Bennet
Dan Boring
Doug Chasse
Joe Duncan
Bob Freeman
John Hooks
Sylvia Hooks
Ted Hooks III
Erma Johns-Lowman
Tom McAfoose
Carol Mikula
Harry Patton
Rita Schaub
Russell Snyder
Diane Stanko
Jack Steffey
Walter Steffey
Dave Tarr
Raymond Tarr
George Venesky
Joyce Whited
Carla Whited-Sims
Doris Whited-Wolfe

And last, but certainly not least, my late aunt Hazel Whited for saving all her old photos.

ABOUT THE AUTHOR

The author, Bob Whited, was born and raised in Bridgeburg, Pennsylvania, a small hamlet with a population of about one hundred, on the Allegheny River near Kittanning. He graduated from Kittanning High school in 1959 and served in the US Navy from 1960 to 1964. He was employed at Haws Refractories in Bridgeburg for two years and then worked at General Motors in Lordstown, Ohio, until his retirement in 1996. Bob has also served as a reporter for various newspapers and has served as a columnist for the Warren (Ohio) *Tribune Chronicle* for the past sixteen years. One of his columns, *Salute on Ship was an Honor*, is in the John F. Kennedy Presidential Library. He has resided in Austintown, Ohio, since 1967 following his marriage to the former Joyce Toussaint of Ford City, Pennsylvania. They have four children, Lisa, Lori, Rob, and Todd. They also have seven grandchildren and two great-grandchildren. Bob is also Past District Governor for Lions Clubs International (Ohio District 13-D, 1995–1996). Bob is also the author of *Navy Grass*, a memoir of his time spent with the US Navy.

CPSIA information can be obtained
at www.ICGtesting.com
Printed in the USA
BVHW091742080321
602014BV00003B/170